The Mindful Gut Journal

A Personal Journal and
a personal journey to support the loving care of a sensitive digestive system.

Reviews

"*The Mindful Gut Journal* is an introspective journaling journey through the various physical, mental, and emotional states encountered during the experience of long-standing digestive disorders. It is wonderful aid in supplementing professional care and provides hope for all those who are living with digestive illness."
- Dr. G. Ramos, Portland, OR

"Marianne Bickett has written a marvelous little handbook for people suffering from digestive disorders. Each creatively illustrated page begins with an affirmation, a nugget of wisdom, followed by specific suggestions for pondering, journaling, or drawing. All of her recommendations offer practical, very doable, steps toward transforming the particular affirmation from just an idea to a lived reality."
-Manuel Costa, MFT, San Jose, CA

"In her journal, Marianne Bickett shares her experiences managing a sensitive digestive system, offering valuable insights and practical strategies that have helped her thrive. This resource aims to support readers in enhancing their well-being and navigating their own digestive health journeys. It is designed to complement, not replace, professional care."
-Colleen Campbell, RPh, Denver, CO

Dedication

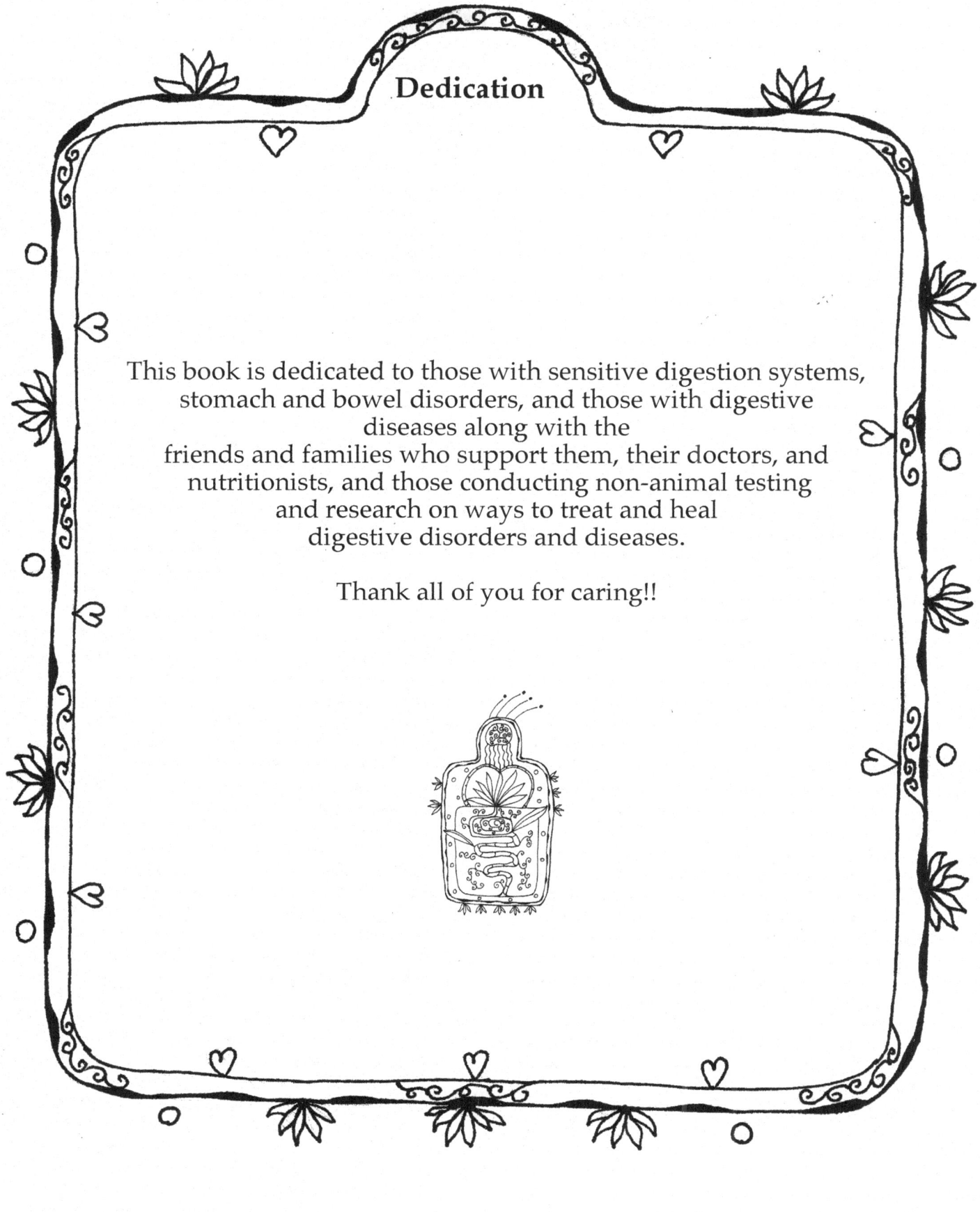

This book is dedicated to those with sensitive digestion systems,
stomach and bowel disorders, and those with digestive
diseases along with the
friends and families who support them, their doctors, and
nutritionists, and those conducting non-animal testing
and research on ways to treat and heal
digestive disorders and diseases.

Thank all of you for caring!!

It is an exciting time to be learning about gut health! There
is a wealth of information (see Resources at the end of this journal)
that is greatly encouraging about building healthy flora
through a varied diet along with stress management strategies.
There is a fascinating, new research about the gut-brain axis
and how our heart, brain, and organs communicate.
Knowledge IS power!

Some statistics to ponder:

The National Institute of Diabetes and Digestive and Kidney Diseases:
IBS prevalence 15.3 million people (1998)
Prescriptions for IBS 5.9 million per year (2004)
GERD prevalence 20% of the population (2004)
Prescriptions for GERD 64.6 million per year (2004)

From Everyday Health, Life with IBS/GERD, 2023:
15% of the world population suffers from IBS with 63% of those also
suffering from GERD.

These statistics don't include the vast number of other digestive diseases
such as IBD*, Crohn's, colitis, and gluten/allergic sensitivities, SIBO/IMO.
The point here is that, looking at IBS and GERD alone, there are millions
of people suffering with digestive ailments.
(*IBD involves inflammation of the colon whereas IBS is a syndrome with a myriad
of symptoms that can be caused by a variety of factors. There are similarities between
the two.)

Author's Note

The intention of this journal is not only to support those with digestive conditions, disorders, and diseases, but also for anyone interested in exploring mind-gut health. Current research indicates that digestive health is paramount to good mental and physical health. Our gut can shape how we feel by how and what we eat. We can change our minds by changing our diets and lifestyle along with working with our emotions and attitudes.

The premise of this journal is that when we become aware of our how our thoughts affect us and the inner struggles that often go untended, we can more effectively manage stomach and gut problems. This is not a cure, but simply an exercise in thoughtful awareness, acceptance, and mindful action. The proverbial "Know Thyself" is very good medicine.

I suggest using this journal in conjunction with professional treatment and guidance by a qualified doctor, and, if possible, a qualified therapist. Please never self-diagnose GERD, IBS or other digestive problems. For example, IBS, SIBO/IMO, and Celiac Sprue have many of the same symptoms. Even an electrolyte imbalance, such as low sodium, can cause nausea and other digestive issues. **Always seek medical attention when needed and follow the advice of your doctors.** I am not a doctor nor medical professional nor a therapist; hence, this book should never be used as a substitute for obtaining consultation or advice from a doctor or health practitioner.

After the initial prompts, there is space to write, draw, color, and/or collage. I invite you to use this journal in any way that serves you best. You can start on any page that invites you to ponder and explore. It can be used sequentially; or begin at the end if you wish! Feel free to color the borders and drawings and add to them with your own images. You may need a sketch pad/additional journaling paper.

This journal is based on my own experiences of dealing with GERD and IBS syndrome. I am sharing prompts and activities that have been therapeutic for me. With new discoveries arising almost daily about the mind-gut relationship, it makes sense to not only treat the physical symptoms as we search for causes, but also to work with the mind. Updated information will be added to this journal from time to time due to the vast amount of new research in this area.

Our perception and our relationship to our bodies can change, we can literally change our minds! Remember, your condition is not in your head, but your thoughts and feelings about your body and your afflictions affect how you heal. Loving acceptance of your unique body, with all its imperfections and qualities, is a vital step to living well. Through my 68 years of living on this beautiful planet, I have learned that everything is connected.

The mind is in the body and the body is the mind. There are many pieces to this vast puzzle of digestive, physical, mental, and emotional health. This book focuses on exploring these aspects via journaling and artmaking. Experiencing chronic stomach problems can greatly affect the quality of our lives. I hope this journal can help to reduce some of the trauma of digestive ailments with explorations of self-awareness and knowledge. And mostly, self-love.

Why fifty-five entries? Well, I was fifty-five when I started this book!!

I heard this wonderful quote recently: "We teach what we need to learn." I have greatly benefitted from the practices in this book and am deeply grateful to be able to share them with you.

May this journal bless you and help you grasp just how *Amazing* you are! *Thank you!*

Guided imagery, body scans, affirmations, and guided meditations can reduce the stress associated with chronic conditions, diseases and disorders. **However, please understand that, for some people who have experienced trauma, doing body scans and working with guided imagery can cause distress. If you feel any discomfort, be gentle and please be sure to work with a qualified somatic therapist.**

I created a You Tube of a *Guided Body Scan*. You can find it by searching for my name on You Tube.

There are also examples of some of the journaling activities on my **website: MarianneBickett.com**

MBickett, Summer 2024

Using the Breath
to calm the sympathetic nervous system
and engage the parasympathetic nervous system:
Breathe in one, two, three, four,
Hold the breath for two counts,
Then breathe out for six counts.
Hold the breath for two counts and then
repeat as many times as needed.

Alternate Nose Breathing:
With your right thumb, hold the right nostril closed.
Breathe in through the left nostril.
Release the right thumb while you
Release the breath through right nostril while you then
Hold the left nostril closed.
Breathe in through the right nostril then close with thumb
While you breathe out through the left nostril.
Repeat this alternating pattern as long as needed to create a
calming effect.

Remember, your condition is not in your head, but your thoughts and feelings about your body and your afflictions affect how you heal. Loving acceptance of your unique body, with all its imperfections and qualities, is a vital step to living well.

For great online mindfulness programs, for beginners to experts, visit the Center for Mindfulness UMASS at:
www.ummhealth.org/center-mindfulness.
I am an alumnus of the program (1991-1993) and it was the first mindfulness based program in the US created by Jon Kabat-Zinn.

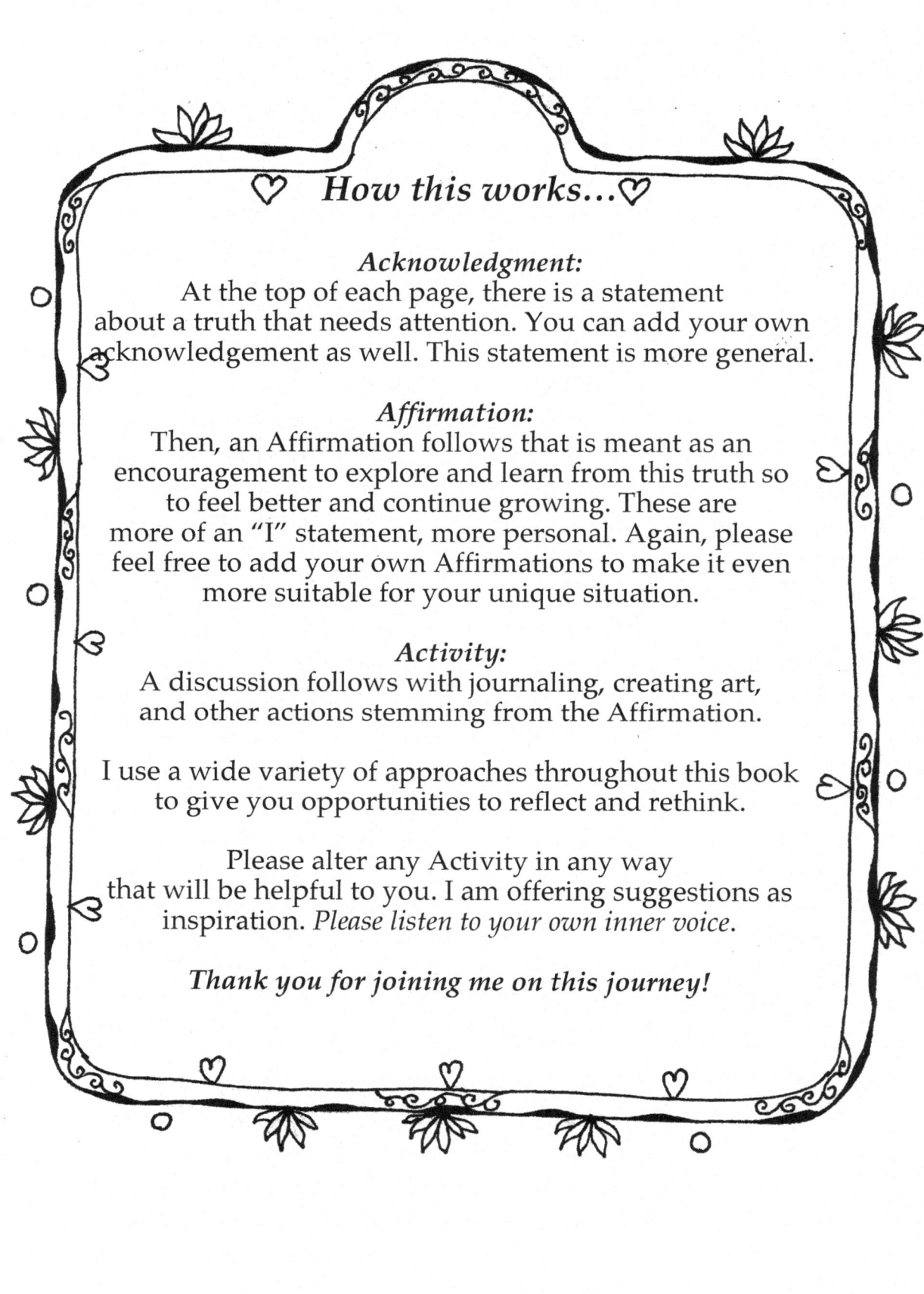

♡ *How this works...* ♡

Acknowledgment:
At the top of each page, there is a statement
about a truth that needs attention. You can add your own
acknowledgement as well. This statement is more general.

Affirmation:
Then, an Affirmation follows that is meant as an
encouragement to explore and learn from this truth so
to feel better and continue growing. These are
more of an "I" statement, more personal. Again, please
feel free to add your own Affirmations to make it even
more suitable for your unique situation.

Activity:
A discussion follows with journaling, creating art,
and other actions stemming from the Affirmation.

I use a wide variety of approaches throughout this book
to give you opportunities to reflect and rethink.

Please alter any Activity in any way
that will be helpful to you. I am offering suggestions as
inspiration. *Please listen to your own inner voice.*

Thank you for joining me on this journey!

Table of Contents

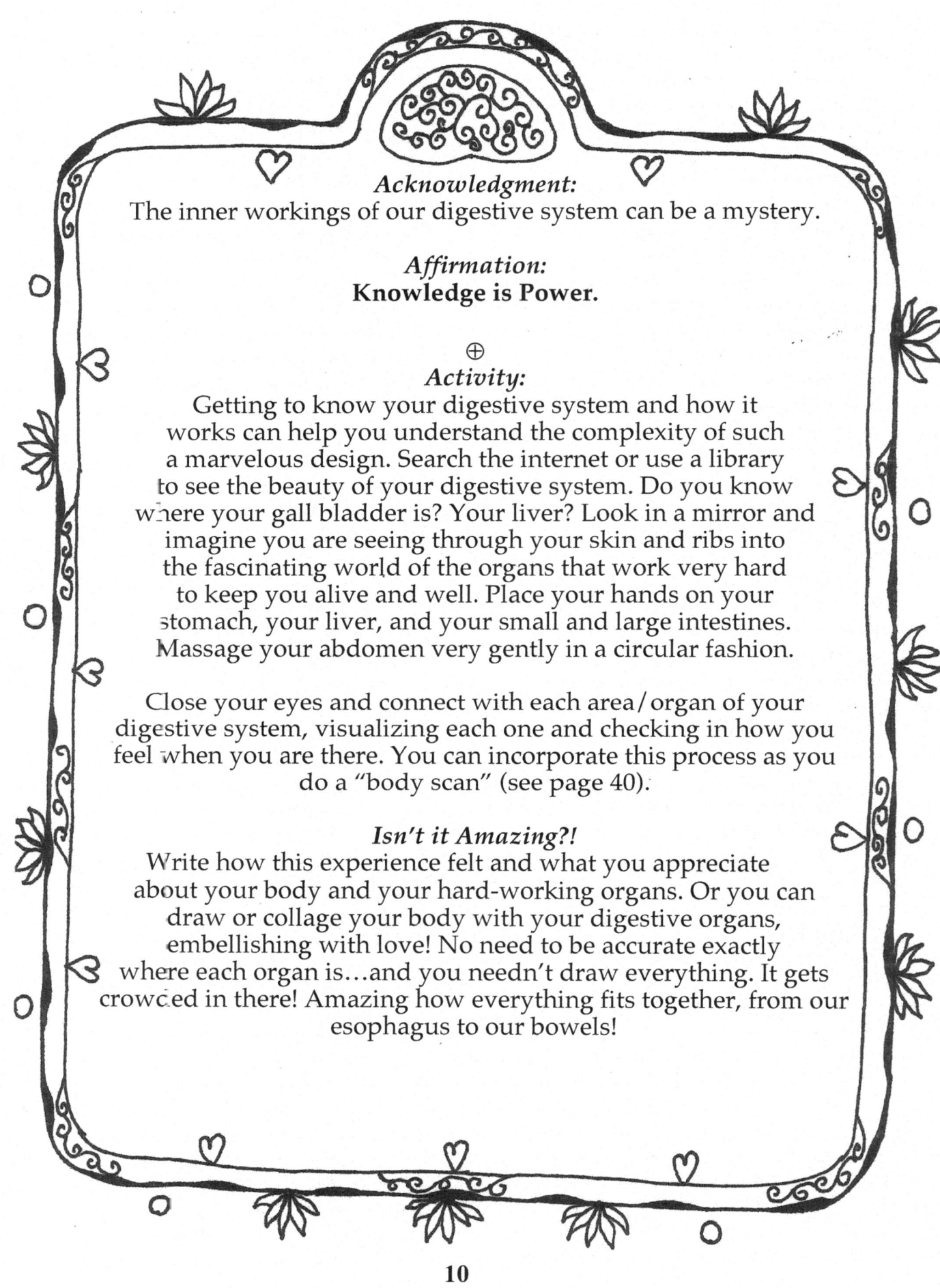

Acknowledgment:
The inner workings of our digestive system can be a mystery.

Affirmation:
Knowledge is Power.

⊕

Activity:
Getting to know your digestive system and how it works can help you understand the complexity of such a marvelous design. Search the internet or use a library to see the beauty of your digestive system. Do you know where your gall bladder is? Your liver? Look in a mirror and imagine you are seeing through your skin and ribs into the fascinating world of the organs that work very hard to keep you alive and well. Place your hands on your stomach, your liver, and your small and large intestines. Massage your abdomen very gently in a circular fashion.

Close your eyes and connect with each area/organ of your digestive system, visualizing each one and checking in how you feel when you are there. You can incorporate this process as you do a "body scan" (see page 40).

Isn't it Amazing?!
Write how this experience felt and what you appreciate about your body and your hard-working organs. Or you can draw or collage your body with your digestive organs, embellishing with love! No need to be accurate exactly where each organ is…and you needn't draw everything. It gets crowded in there! Amazing how everything fits together, from our esophagus to our bowels!

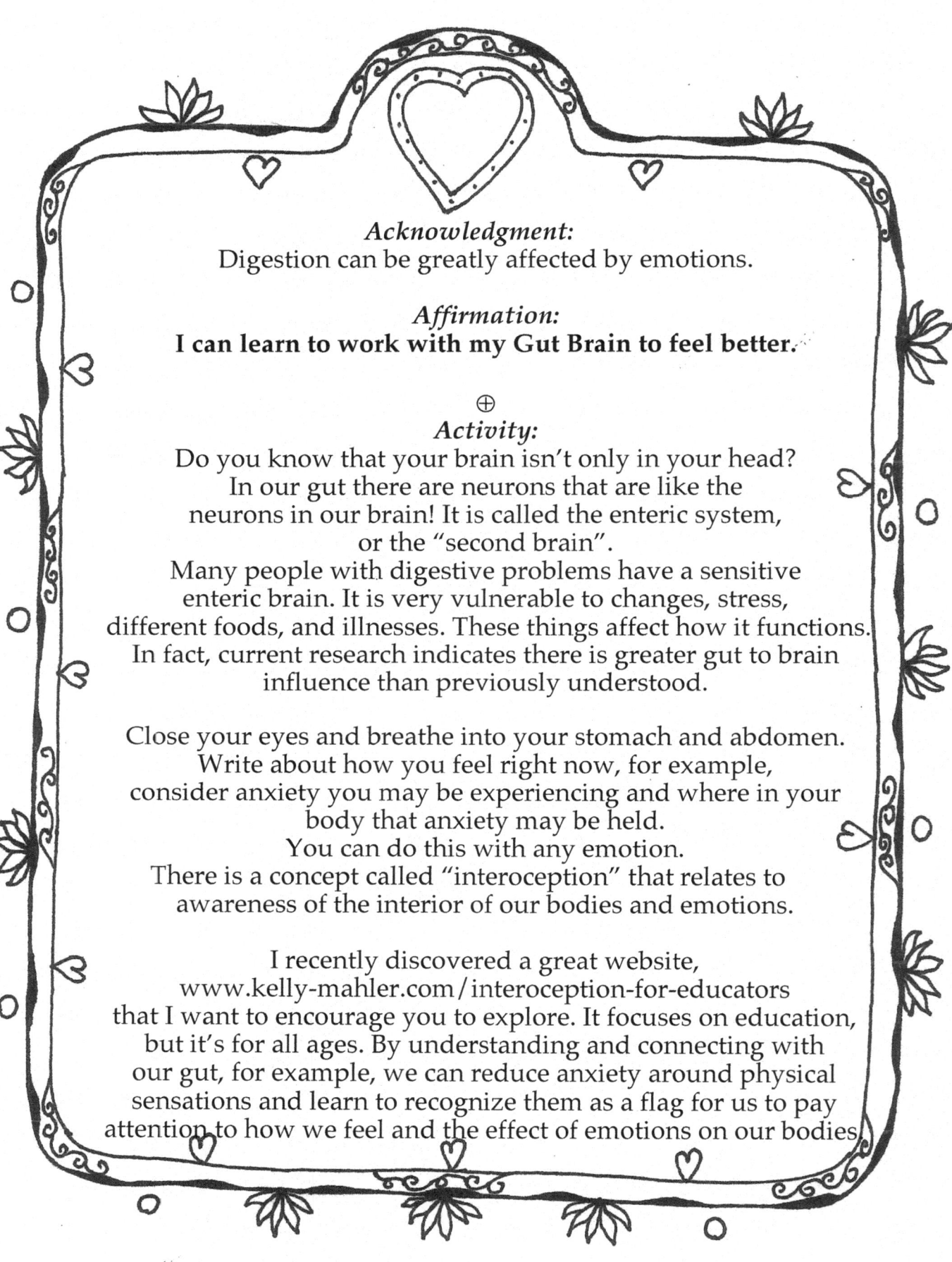

Acknowledgment:
Digestion can be greatly affected by emotions.

Affirmation:
I can learn to work with my Gut Brain to feel better.

⊕

Activity:
Do you know that your brain isn't only in your head?
In our gut there are neurons that are like the
neurons in our brain! It is called the enteric system,
or the "second brain".
Many people with digestive problems have a sensitive
enteric brain. It is very vulnerable to changes, stress,
different foods, and illnesses. These things affect how it functions.
In fact, current research indicates there is greater gut to brain
influence than previously understood.

Close your eyes and breathe into your stomach and abdomen.
Write about how you feel right now, for example,
consider anxiety you may be experiencing and where in your
body that anxiety may be held.
You can do this with any emotion.
There is a concept called "interoception" that relates to
awareness of the interior of our bodies and emotions.

I recently discovered a great website,
www.kelly-mahler.com/interoception-for-educators
that I want to encourage you to explore. It focuses on education,
but it's for all ages. By understanding and connecting with
our gut, for example, we can reduce anxiety around physical
sensations and learn to recognize them as a flag for us to pay
attention to how we feel and the effect of emotions on our bodies

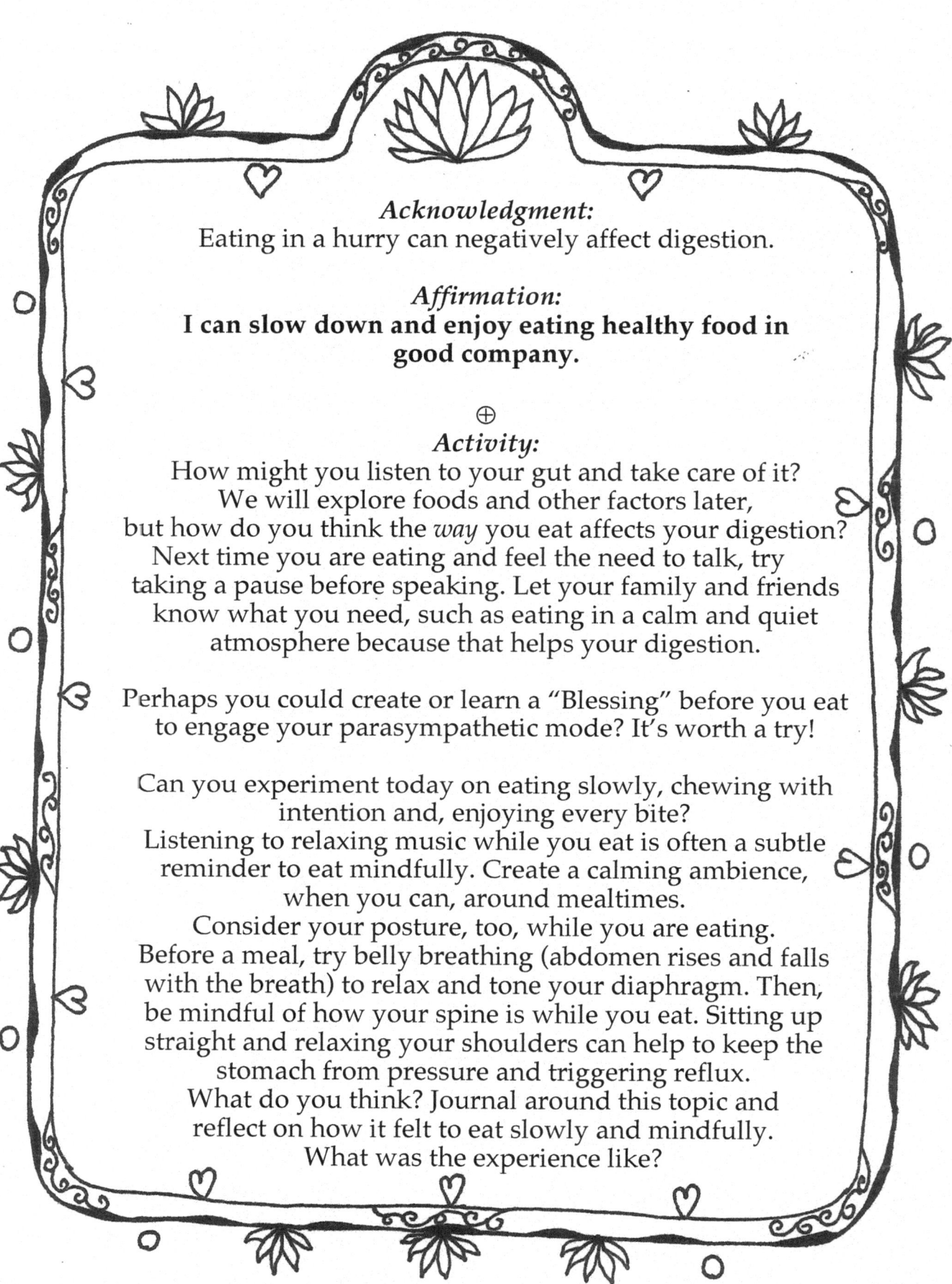

Acknowledgment:
Eating in a hurry can negatively affect digestion.

Affirmation:
I can slow down and enjoy eating healthy food in good company.

⊕

Activity:
How might you listen to your gut and take care of it?
We will explore foods and other factors later,
but how do you think the *way* you eat affects your digestion?
Next time you are eating and feel the need to talk, try
taking a pause before speaking. Let your family and friends
know what you need, such as eating in a calm and quiet
atmosphere because that helps your digestion.

Perhaps you could create or learn a "Blessing" before you eat
to engage your parasympathetic mode? It's worth a try!

Can you experiment today on eating slowly, chewing with
intention and, enjoying every bite?
Listening to relaxing music while you eat is often a subtle
reminder to eat mindfully. Create a calming ambience,
when you can, around mealtimes.
Consider your posture, too, while you are eating.
Before a meal, try belly breathing (abdomen rises and falls
with the breath) to relax and tone your diaphragm. Then,
be mindful of how your spine is while you eat. Sitting up
straight and relaxing your shoulders can help to keep the
stomach from pressure and triggering reflux.
What do you think? Journal around this topic and
reflect on how it felt to eat slowly and mindfully.
What was the experience like?

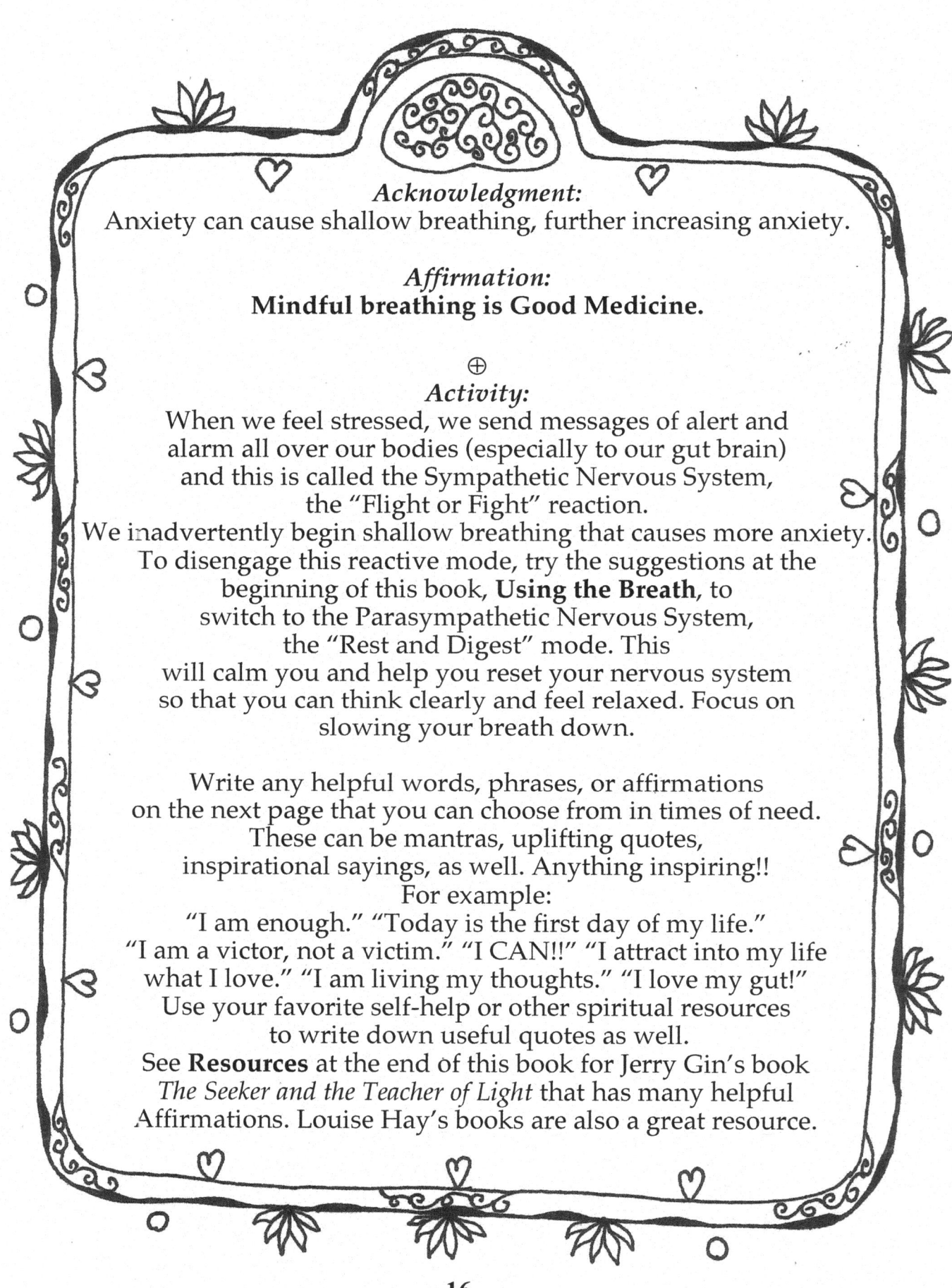

Acknowledgment:
Anxiety can cause shallow breathing, further increasing anxiety.

Affirmation:
Mindful breathing is Good Medicine.

⊕

Activity:
When we feel stressed, we send messages of alert and
alarm all over our bodies (especially to our gut brain)
and this is called the Sympathetic Nervous System,
the "Flight or Fight" reaction.
We inadvertently begin shallow breathing that causes more anxiety.
To disengage this reactive mode, try the suggestions at the
beginning of this book, **Using the Breath**, to
switch to the Parasympathetic Nervous System,
the "Rest and Digest" mode. This
will calm you and help you reset your nervous system
so that you can think clearly and feel relaxed. Focus on
slowing your breath down.

Write any helpful words, phrases, or affirmations
on the next page that you can choose from in times of need.
These can be mantras, uplifting quotes,
inspirational sayings, as well. Anything inspiring!!
For example:
"I am enough." "Today is the first day of my life."
"I am a victor, not a victim." "I CAN!!" "I attract into my life
what I love." "I am living my thoughts." "I love my gut!"
Use your favorite self-help or other spiritual resources
to write down useful quotes as well.
See **Resources** at the end of this book for Jerry Gin's book
The Seeker and the Teacher of Light that has many helpful
Affirmations. Louise Hay's books are also a great resource.

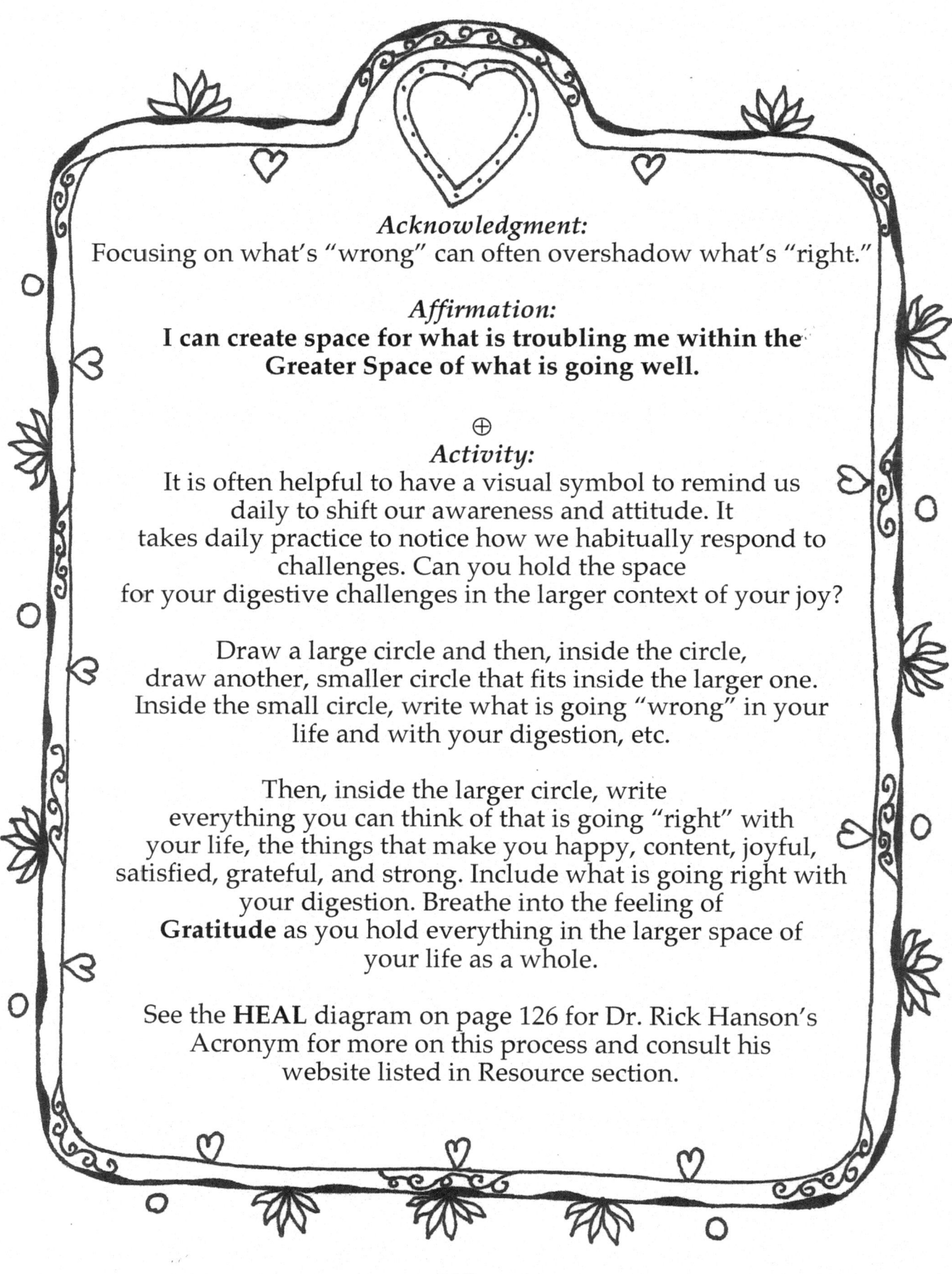

Acknowledgment:
Focusing on what's "wrong" can often overshadow what's "right."

Affirmation:
I can create space for what is troubling me within the Greater Space of what is going well.

⊕

Activity:
It is often helpful to have a visual symbol to remind us daily to shift our awareness and attitude. It takes daily practice to notice how we habitually respond to challenges. Can you hold the space for your digestive challenges in the larger context of your joy?

Draw a large circle and then, inside the circle, draw another, smaller circle that fits inside the larger one. Inside the small circle, write what is going "wrong" in your life and with your digestion, etc.

Then, inside the larger circle, write everything you can think of that is going "right" with your life, the things that make you happy, content, joyful, satisfied, grateful, and strong. Include what is going right with your digestion. Breathe into the feeling of **Gratitude** as you hold everything in the larger space of your life as a whole.

See the **HEAL** diagram on page 126 for Dr. Rick Hanson's Acronym for more on this process and consult his website listed in Resource section.

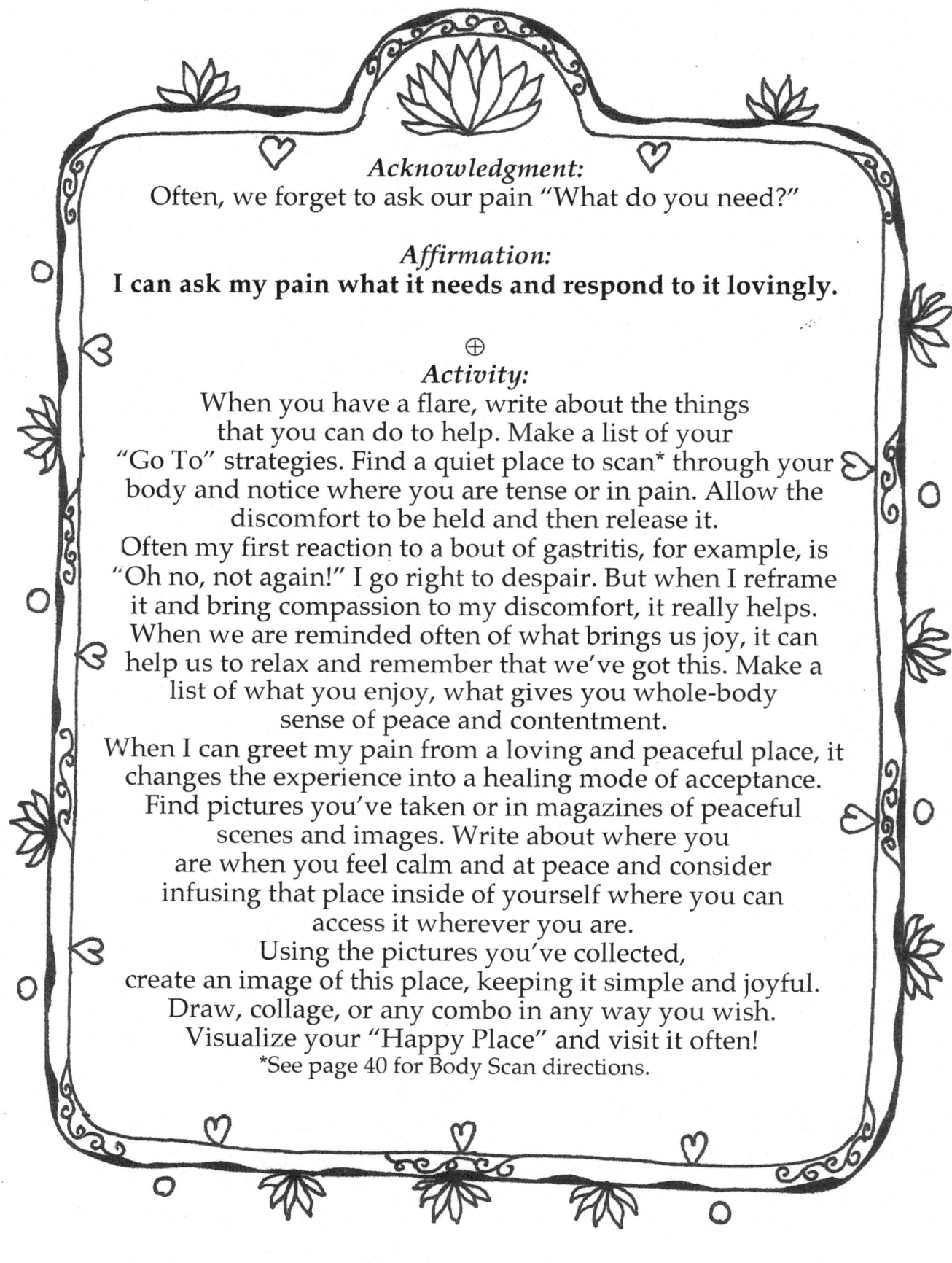

Acknowledgment:
Often, we forget to ask our pain "What do you need?"

Affirmation:
I can ask my pain what it needs and respond to it lovingly.

⊕

Activity:
When you have a flare, write about the things
that you can do to help. Make a list of your
"Go To" strategies. Find a quiet place to scan* through your
body and notice where you are tense or in pain. Allow the
discomfort to be held and then release it.
Often my first reaction to a bout of gastritis, for example, is
"Oh no, not again!" I go right to despair. But when I reframe
it and bring compassion to my discomfort, it really helps.
When we are reminded often of what brings us joy, it can
help us to relax and remember that we've got this. Make a
list of what you enjoy, what gives you whole-body
sense of peace and contentment.
When I can greet my pain from a loving and peaceful place, it
changes the experience into a healing mode of acceptance.
Find pictures you've taken or in magazines of peaceful
scenes and images. Write about where you
are when you feel calm and at peace and consider
infusing that place inside of yourself where you can
access it wherever you are.
Using the pictures you've collected,
create an image of this place, keeping it simple and joyful.
Draw, collage, or any combo in any way you wish.
Visualize your "Happy Place" and visit it often!
*See page 40 for Body Scan directions.

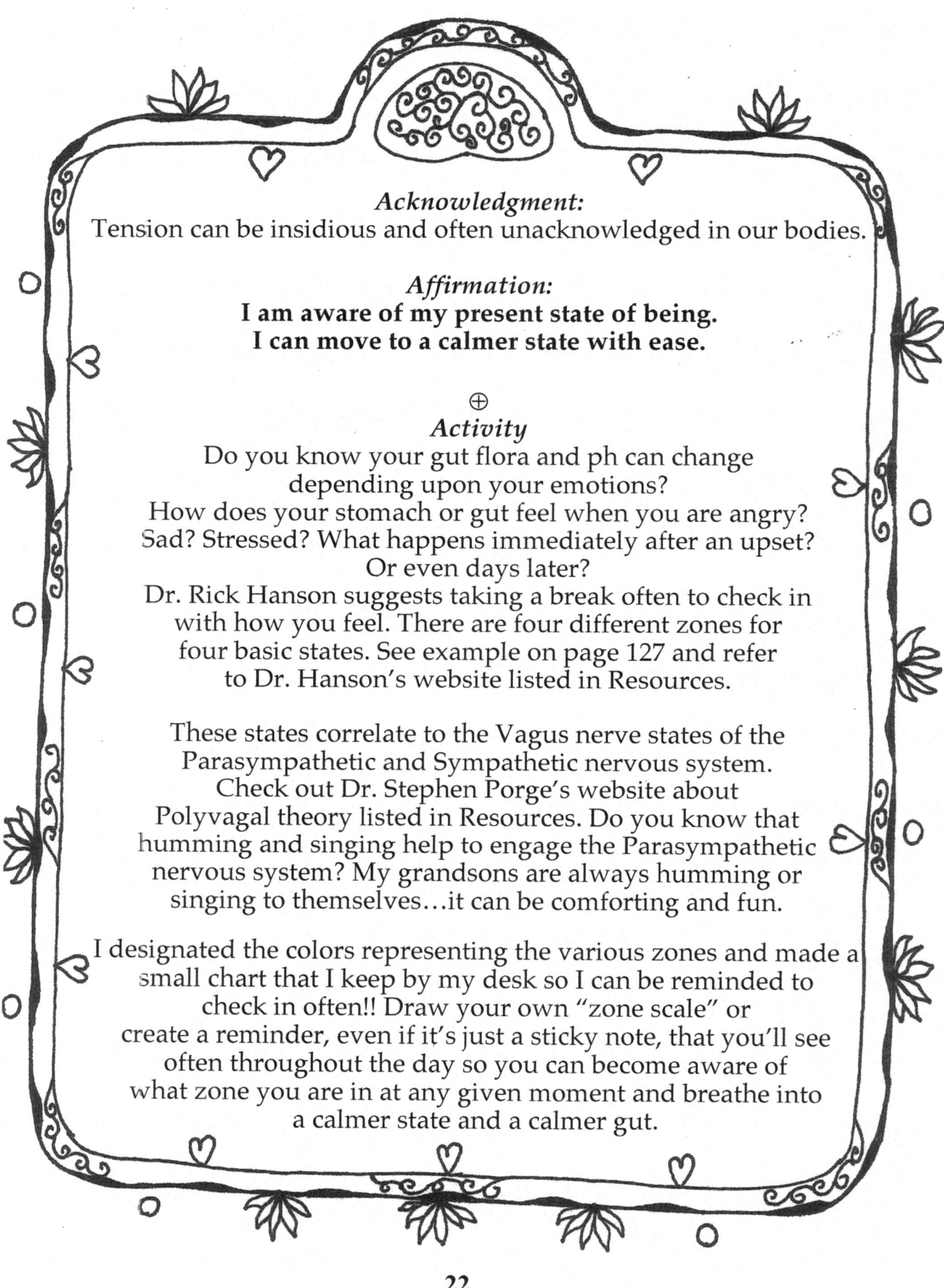

Acknowledgment:
Tension can be insidious and often unacknowledged in our bodies.

Affirmation:
I am aware of my present state of being.
I can move to a calmer state with ease.

⊕

Activity
Do you know your gut flora and ph can change
depending upon your emotions?
How does your stomach or gut feel when you are angry?
Sad? Stressed? What happens immediately after an upset?
Or even days later?
Dr. Rick Hanson suggests taking a break often to check in
with how you feel. There are four different zones for
four basic states. See example on page 127 and refer
to Dr. Hanson's website listed in Resources.

These states correlate to the Vagus nerve states of the
Parasympathetic and Sympathetic nervous system.
Check out Dr. Stephen Porge's website about
Polyvagal theory listed in Resources. Do you know that
humming and singing help to engage the Parasympathetic
nervous system? My grandsons are always humming or
singing to themselves...it can be comforting and fun.

I designated the colors representing the various zones and made a
small chart that I keep by my desk so I can be reminded to
check in often!! Draw your own "zone scale" or
create a reminder, even if it's just a sticky note, that you'll see
often throughout the day so you can become aware of
what zone you are in at any given moment and breathe into
a calmer state and a calmer gut.

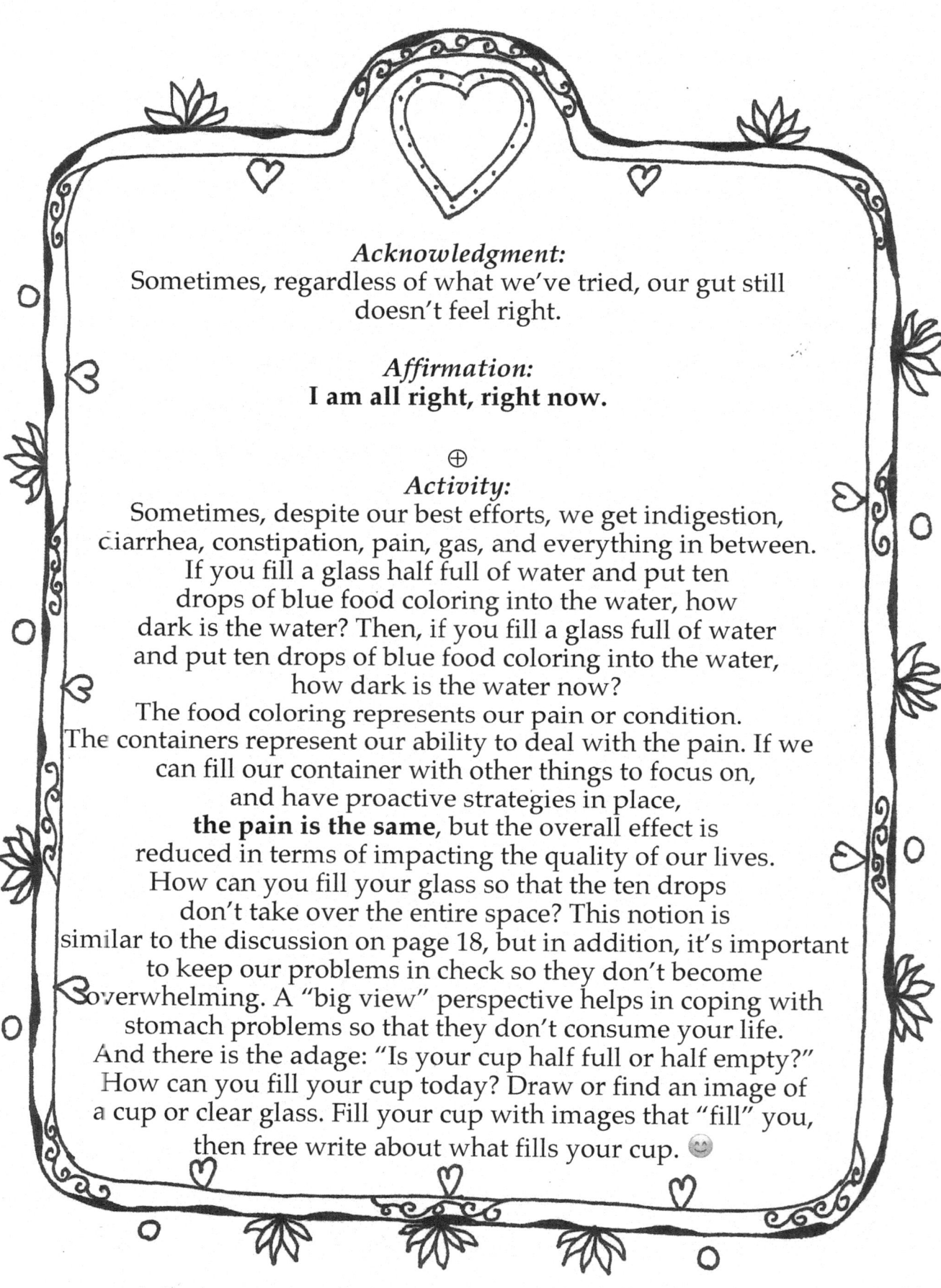

Acknowledgment:
Sometimes, regardless of what we've tried, our gut still
doesn't feel right.

Affirmation:
I am all right, right now.

⊕

Activity:
Sometimes, despite our best efforts, we get indigestion,
diarrhea, constipation, pain, gas, and everything in between.
If you fill a glass half full of water and put ten
drops of blue food coloring into the water, how
dark is the water? Then, if you fill a glass full of water
and put ten drops of blue food coloring into the water,
how dark is the water now?
The food coloring represents our pain or condition.
The containers represent our ability to deal with the pain. If we
can fill our container with other things to focus on,
and have proactive strategies in place,
the pain is the same, but the overall effect is
reduced in terms of impacting the quality of our lives.
How can you fill your glass so that the ten drops
don't take over the entire space? This notion is
similar to the discussion on page 18, but in addition, it's important
to keep our problems in check so they don't become
overwhelming. A "big view" perspective helps in coping with
stomach problems so that they don't consume your life.
And there is the adage: "Is your cup half full or half empty?"
How can you fill your cup today? Draw or find an image of
a cup or clear glass. Fill your cup with images that "fill" you,
then free write about what fills your cup. 😊

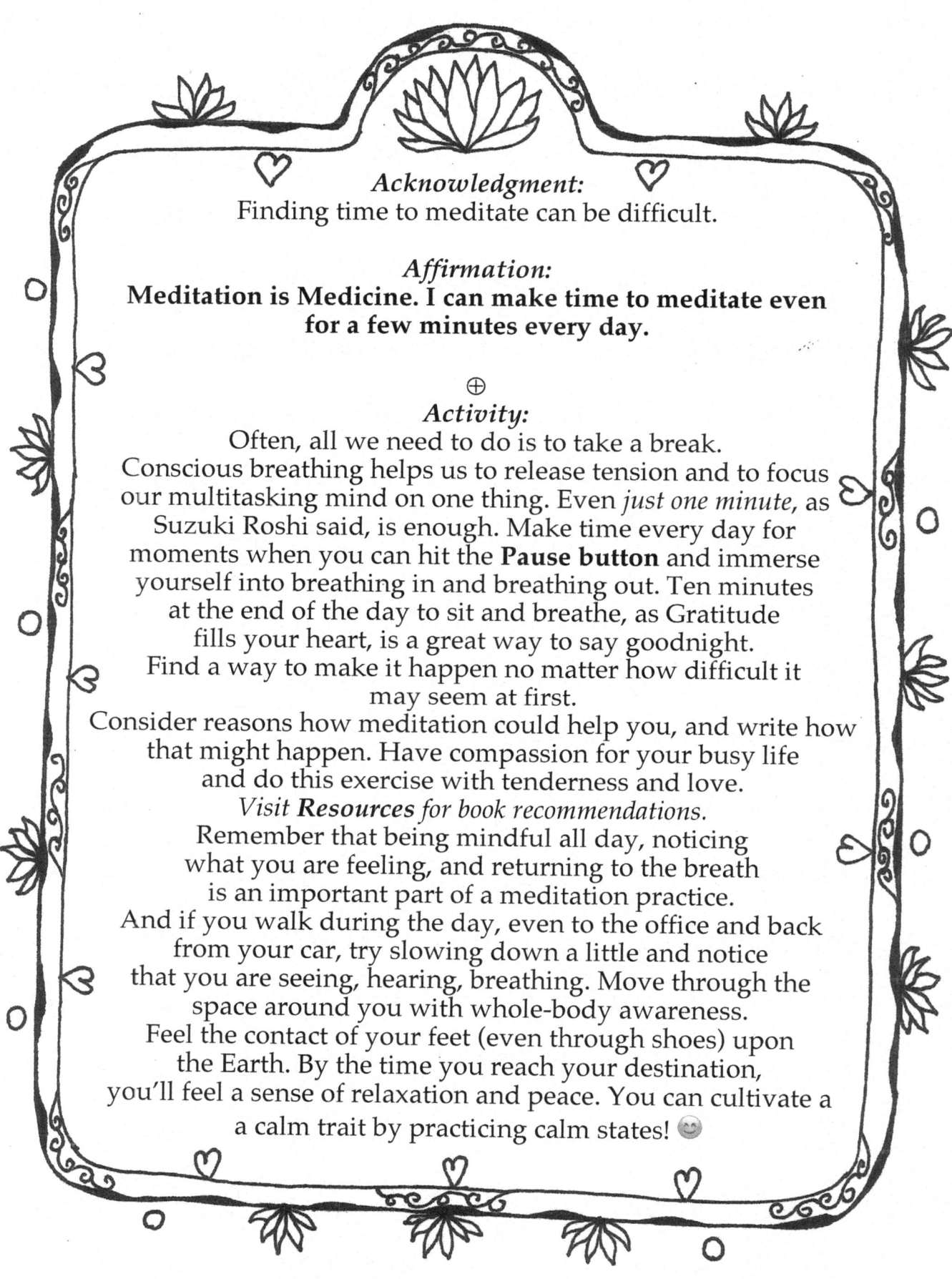

Acknowledgment:
Finding time to meditate can be difficult.

Affirmation:
**Meditation is Medicine. I can make time to meditate even
for a few minutes every day.**

⊕

Activity:
Often, all we need to do is to take a break.
Conscious breathing helps us to release tension and to focus
our multitasking mind on one thing. Even *just one minute*, as
Suzuki Roshi said, is enough. Make time every day for
moments when you can hit the **Pause button** and immerse
yourself into breathing in and breathing out. Ten minutes
at the end of the day to sit and breathe, as Gratitude
fills your heart, is a great way to say goodnight.
Find a way to make it happen no matter how difficult it
may seem at first.
Consider reasons how meditation could help you, and write how
that might happen. Have compassion for your busy life
and do this exercise with tenderness and love.
*Visit **Resources** for book recommendations.*
Remember that being mindful all day, noticing
what you are feeling, and returning to the breath
is an important part of a meditation practice.
And if you walk during the day, even to the office and back
from your car, try slowing down a little and notice
that you are seeing, hearing, breathing. Move through the
space around you with whole-body awareness.
Feel the contact of your feet (even through shoes) upon
the Earth. By the time you reach your destination,
you'll feel a sense of relaxation and peace. You can cultivate a
a calm trait by practicing calm states! 😊

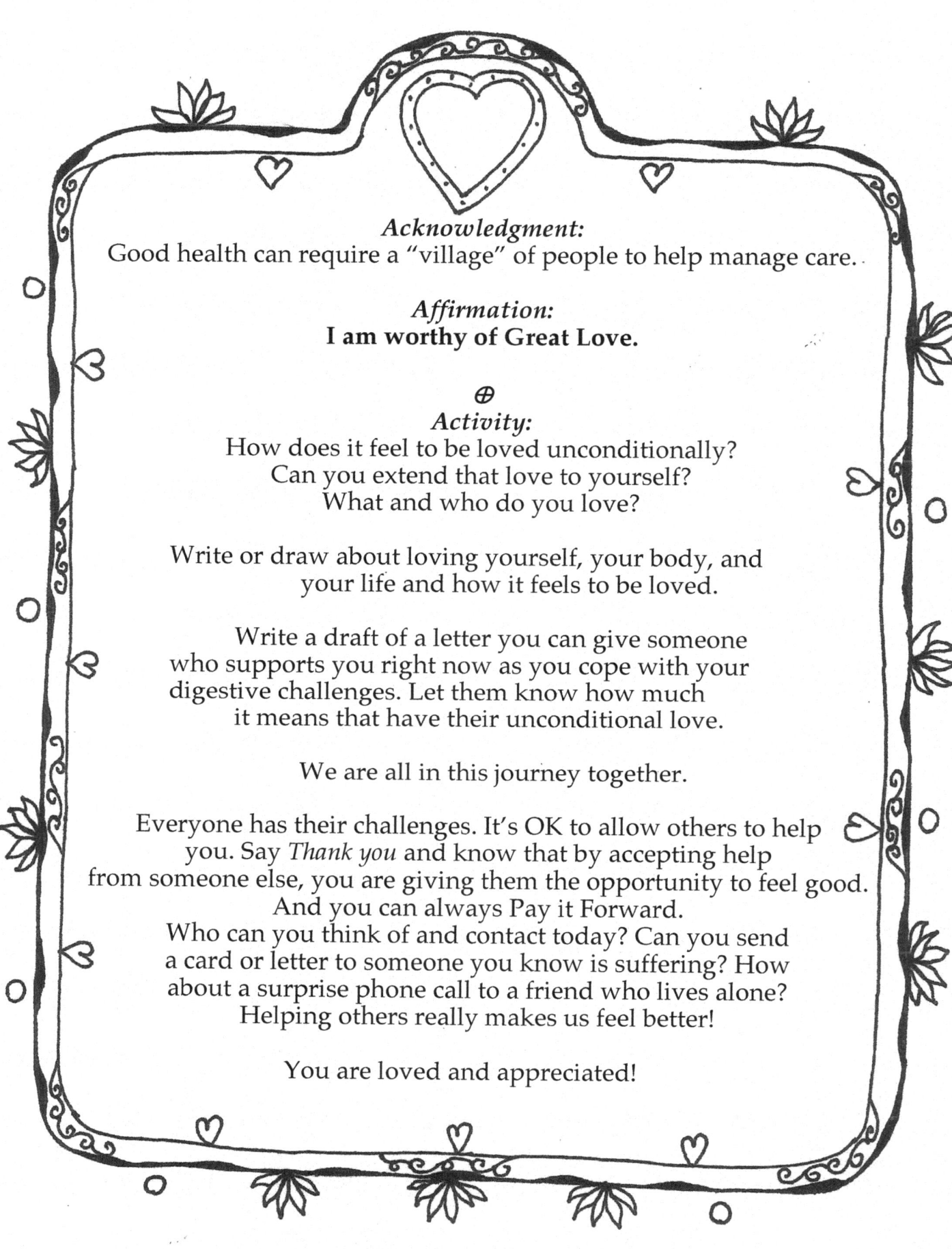

Acknowledgment:
Good health can require a "village" of people to help manage care.

Affirmation:
I am worthy of Great Love.

⊕

Activity:
How does it feel to be loved unconditionally?
Can you extend that love to yourself?
What and who do you love?

Write or draw about loving yourself, your body, and
your life and how it feels to be loved.

Write a draft of a letter you can give someone
who supports you right now as you cope with your
digestive challenges. Let them know how much
it means that have their unconditional love.

We are all in this journey together.

Everyone has their challenges. It's OK to allow others to help
you. Say *Thank you* and know that by accepting help
from someone else, you are giving them the opportunity to feel good.
And you can always Pay it Forward.
Who can you think of and contact today? Can you send
a card or letter to someone you know is suffering? How
about a surprise phone call to a friend who lives alone?
Helping others really makes us feel better!

You are loved and appreciated!

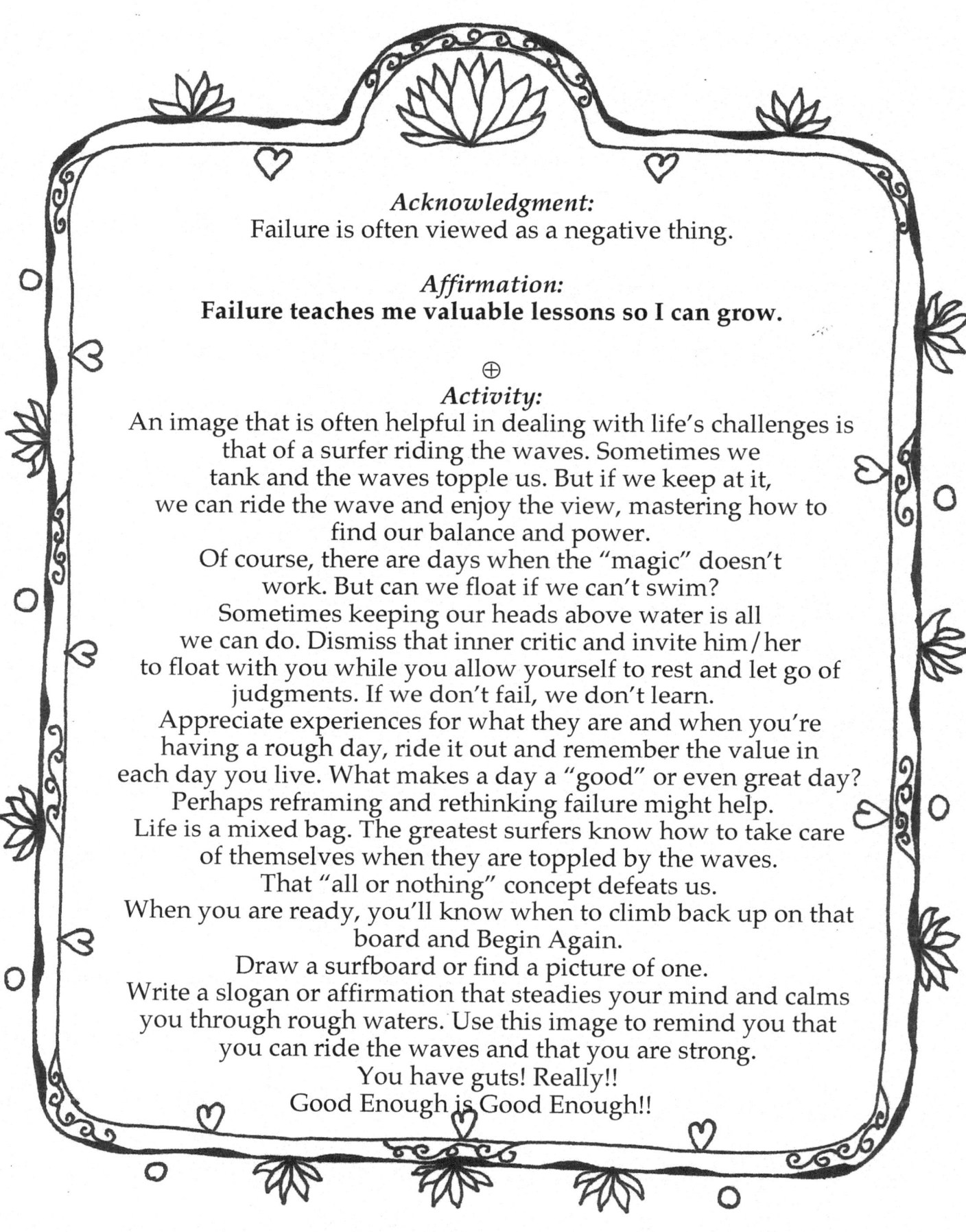

Acknowledgment:
Failure is often viewed as a negative thing.

Affirmation:
Failure teaches me valuable lessons so I can grow.

⊕

Activity:
An image that is often helpful in dealing with life's challenges is
that of a surfer riding the waves. Sometimes we
tank and the waves topple us. But if we keep at it,
we can ride the wave and enjoy the view, mastering how to
find our balance and power.
Of course, there are days when the "magic" doesn't
work. But can we float if we can't swim?
Sometimes keeping our heads above water is all
we can do. Dismiss that inner critic and invite him/her
to float with you while you allow yourself to rest and let go of
judgments. If we don't fail, we don't learn.
Appreciate experiences for what they are and when you're
having a rough day, ride it out and remember the value in
each day you live. What makes a day a "good" or even great day?
Perhaps reframing and rethinking failure might help.
Life is a mixed bag. The greatest surfers know how to take care
of themselves when they are toppled by the waves.
That "all or nothing" concept defeats us.
When you are ready, you'll know when to climb back up on that
board and Begin Again.
Draw a surfboard or find a picture of one.
Write a slogan or affirmation that steadies your mind and calms
you through rough waters. Use this image to remind you that
you can ride the waves and that you are strong.
You have guts! Really!!
Good Enough is Good Enough!!

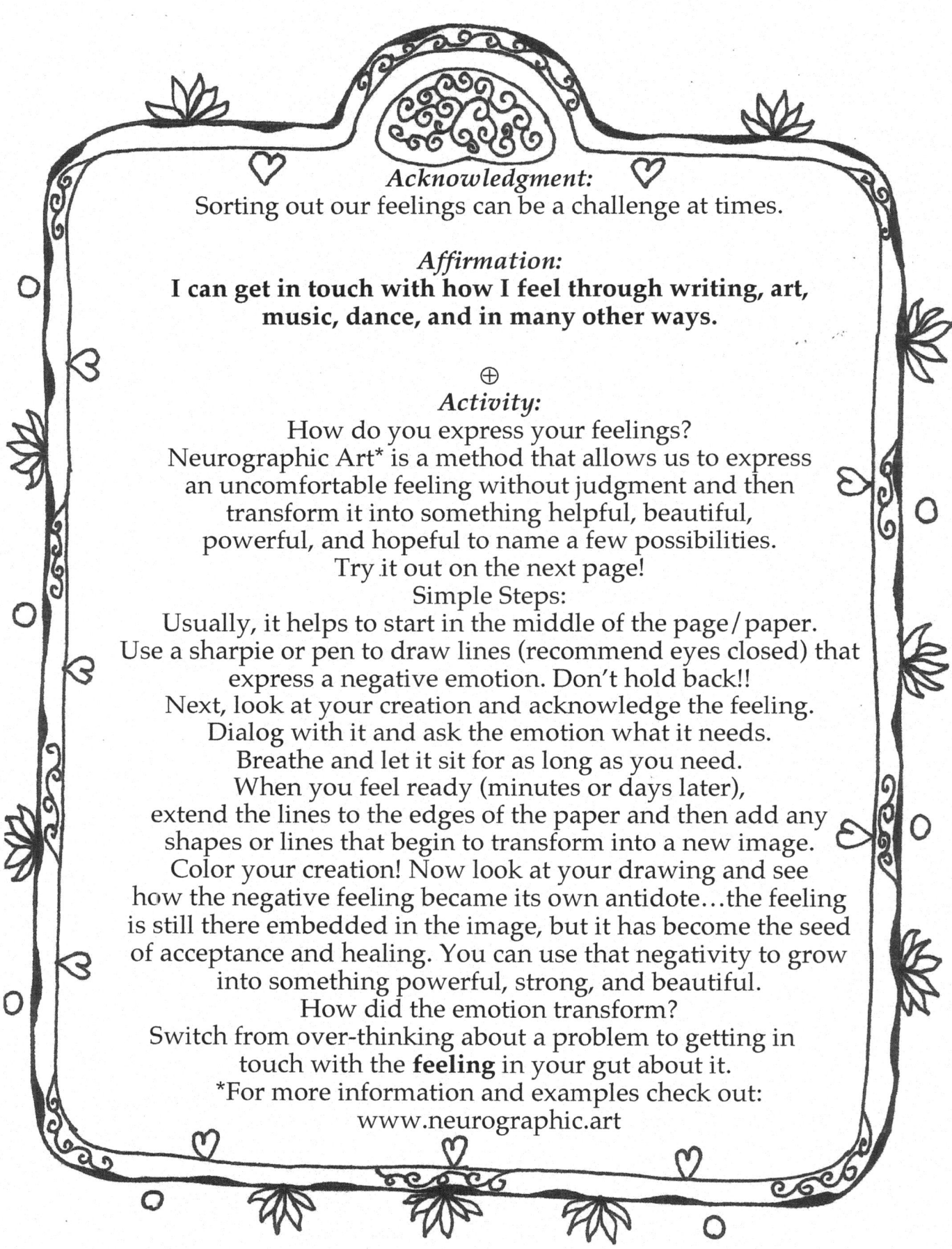

Acknowledgment:
Sorting out our feelings can be a challenge at times.

Affirmation:
I can get in touch with how I feel through writing, art, music, dance, and in many other ways.

⊕

Activity:
How do you express your feelings?
Neurographic Art* is a method that allows us to express
an uncomfortable feeling without judgment and then
transform it into something helpful, beautiful,
powerful, and hopeful to name a few possibilities.
Try it out on the next page!
Simple Steps:
Usually, it helps to start in the middle of the page/paper.
Use a sharpie or pen to draw lines (recommend eyes closed) that
express a negative emotion. Don't hold back!!
Next, look at your creation and acknowledge the feeling.
Dialog with it and ask the emotion what it needs.
Breathe and let it sit for as long as you need.
When you feel ready (minutes or days later),
extend the lines to the edges of the paper and then add any
shapes or lines that begin to transform into a new image.
Color your creation! Now look at your drawing and see
how the negative feeling became its own antidote...the feeling
is still there embedded in the image, but it has become the seed
of acceptance and healing. You can use that negativity to grow
into something powerful, strong, and beautiful.
How did the emotion transform?
Switch from over-thinking about a problem to getting in
touch with the **feeling** in your gut about it.
*For more information and examples check out:
www.neurographic.art

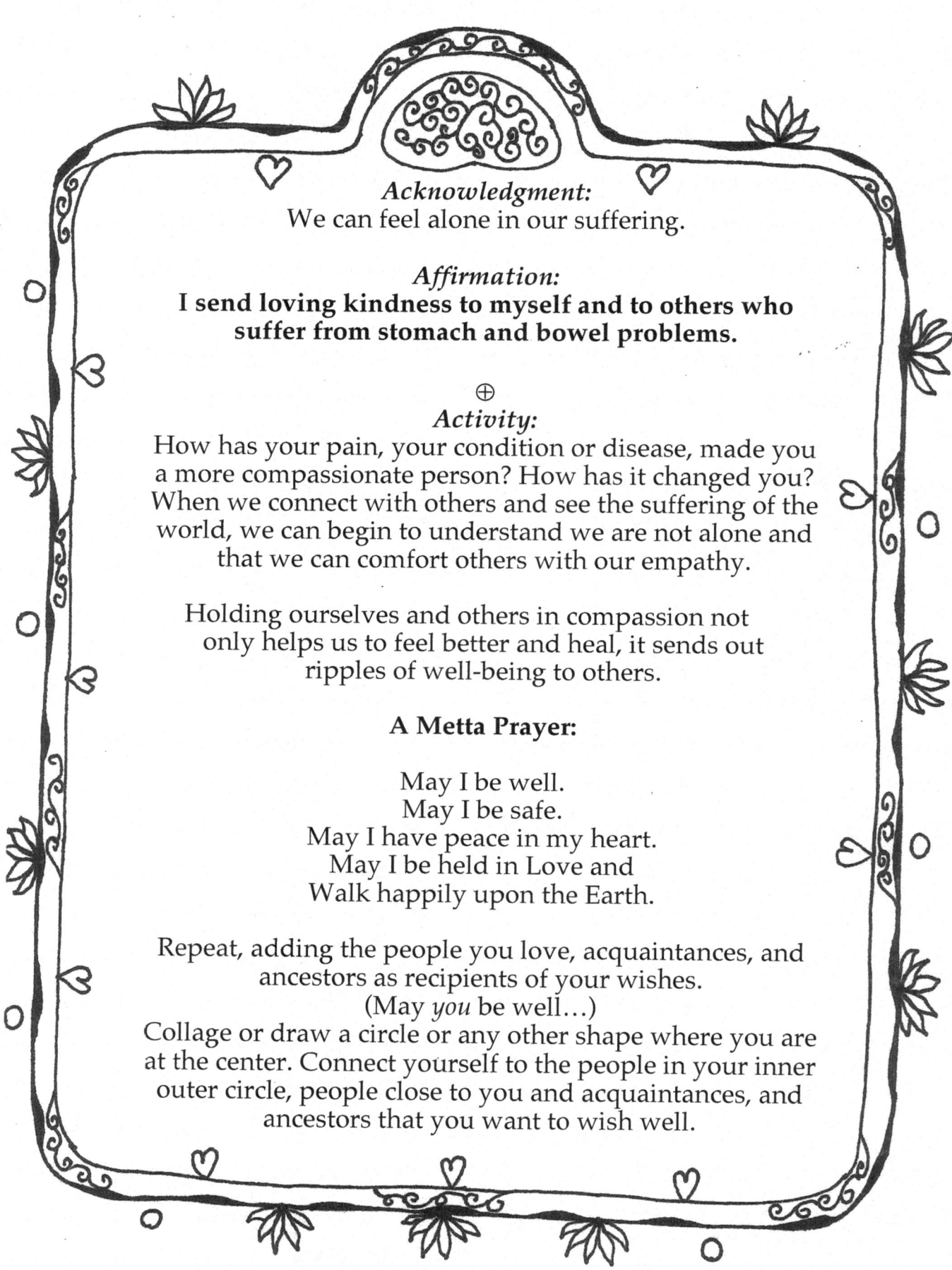

Acknowledgment:
We can feel alone in our suffering.

Affirmation:
I send loving kindness to myself and to others who suffer from stomach and bowel problems.

⊕
Activity:
How has your pain, your condition or disease, made you a more compassionate person? How has it changed you? When we connect with others and see the suffering of the world, we can begin to understand we are not alone and that we can comfort others with our empathy.

Holding ourselves and others in compassion not only helps us to feel better and heal, it sends out ripples of well-being to others.

A Metta Prayer:

May I be well.
May I be safe.
May I have peace in my heart.
May I be held in Love and
Walk happily upon the Earth.

Repeat, adding the people you love, acquaintances, and ancestors as recipients of your wishes.
(May *you* be well...)
Collage or draw a circle or any other shape where you are at the center. Connect yourself to the people in your inner outer circle, people close to you and acquaintances, and ancestors that you want to wish well.

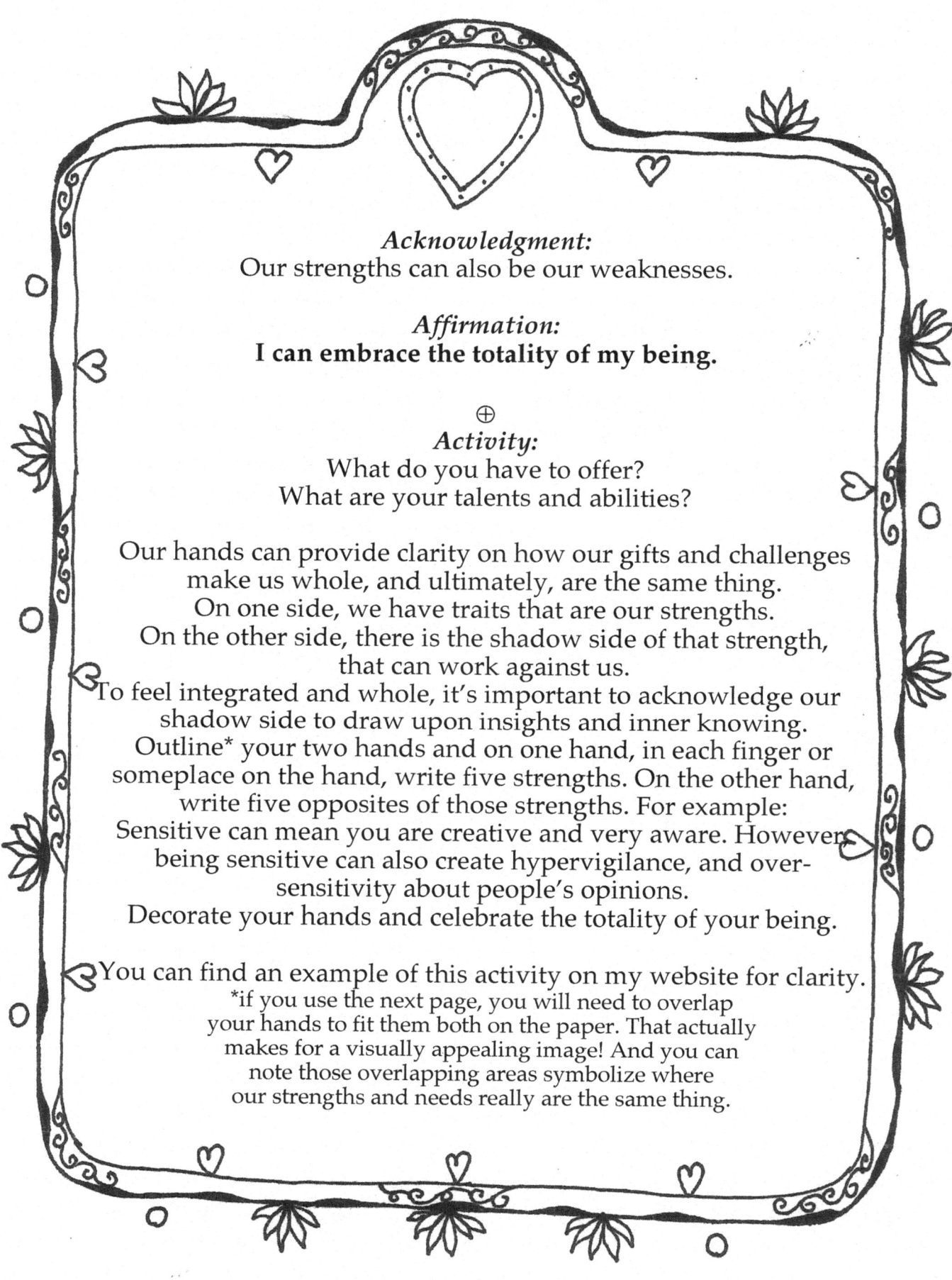

Acknowledgment:
Our strengths can also be our weaknesses.

Affirmation:
I can embrace the totality of my being.

⊕

Activity:
What do you have to offer?
What are your talents and abilities?

Our hands can provide clarity on how our gifts and challenges
make us whole, and ultimately, are the same thing.
On one side, we have traits that are our strengths.
On the other side, there is the shadow side of that strength,
that can work against us.
To feel integrated and whole, it's important to acknowledge our
shadow side to draw upon insights and inner knowing.
Outline* your two hands and on one hand, in each finger or
someplace on the hand, write five strengths. On the other hand,
write five opposites of those strengths. For example:
Sensitive can mean you are creative and very aware. However,
being sensitive can also create hypervigilance, and over-
sensitivity about people's opinions.
Decorate your hands and celebrate the totality of your being.

You can find an example of this activity on my website for clarity.
*if you use the next page, you will need to overlap
your hands to fit them both on the paper. That actually
makes for a visually appealing image! And you can
note those overlapping areas symbolize where
our strengths and needs really are the same thing.

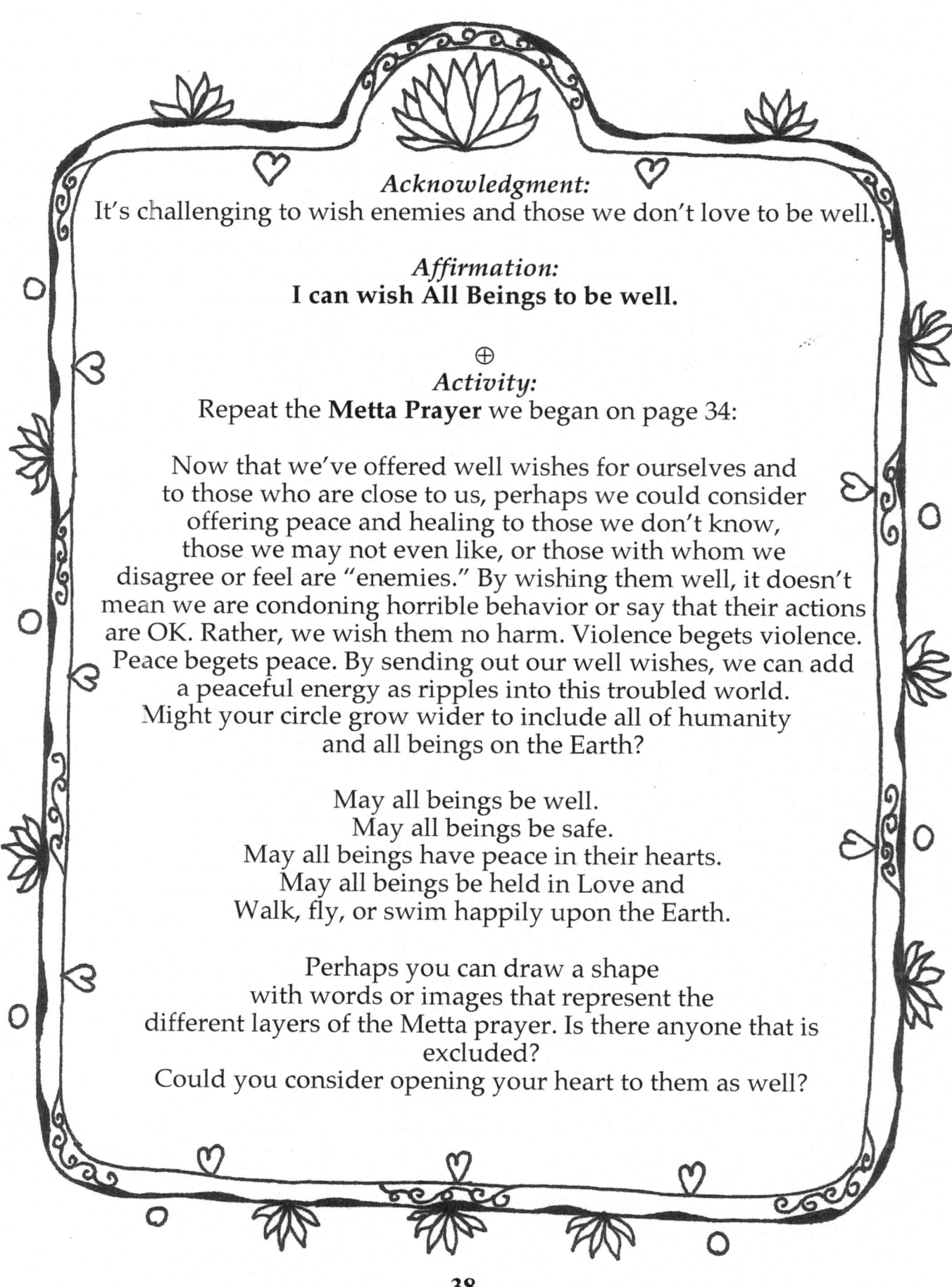

Acknowledgment:
It's challenging to wish enemies and those we don't love to be well.

Affirmation:
I can wish All Beings to be well.

⊕

Activity:
Repeat the **Metta Prayer** we began on page 34:

Now that we've offered well wishes for ourselves and
to those who are close to us, perhaps we could consider
offering peace and healing to those we don't know,
those we may not even like, or those with whom we
disagree or feel are "enemies." By wishing them well, it doesn't
mean we are condoning horrible behavior or say that their actions
are OK. Rather, we wish them no harm. Violence begets violence.
Peace begets peace. By sending out our well wishes, we can add
a peaceful energy as ripples into this troubled world.
Might your circle grow wider to include all of humanity
and all beings on the Earth?

May all beings be well.
May all beings be safe.
May all beings have peace in their hearts.
May all beings be held in Love and
Walk, fly, or swim happily upon the Earth.

Perhaps you can draw a shape
with words or images that represent the
different layers of the Metta prayer. Is there anyone that is
excluded?
Could you consider opening your heart to them as well?

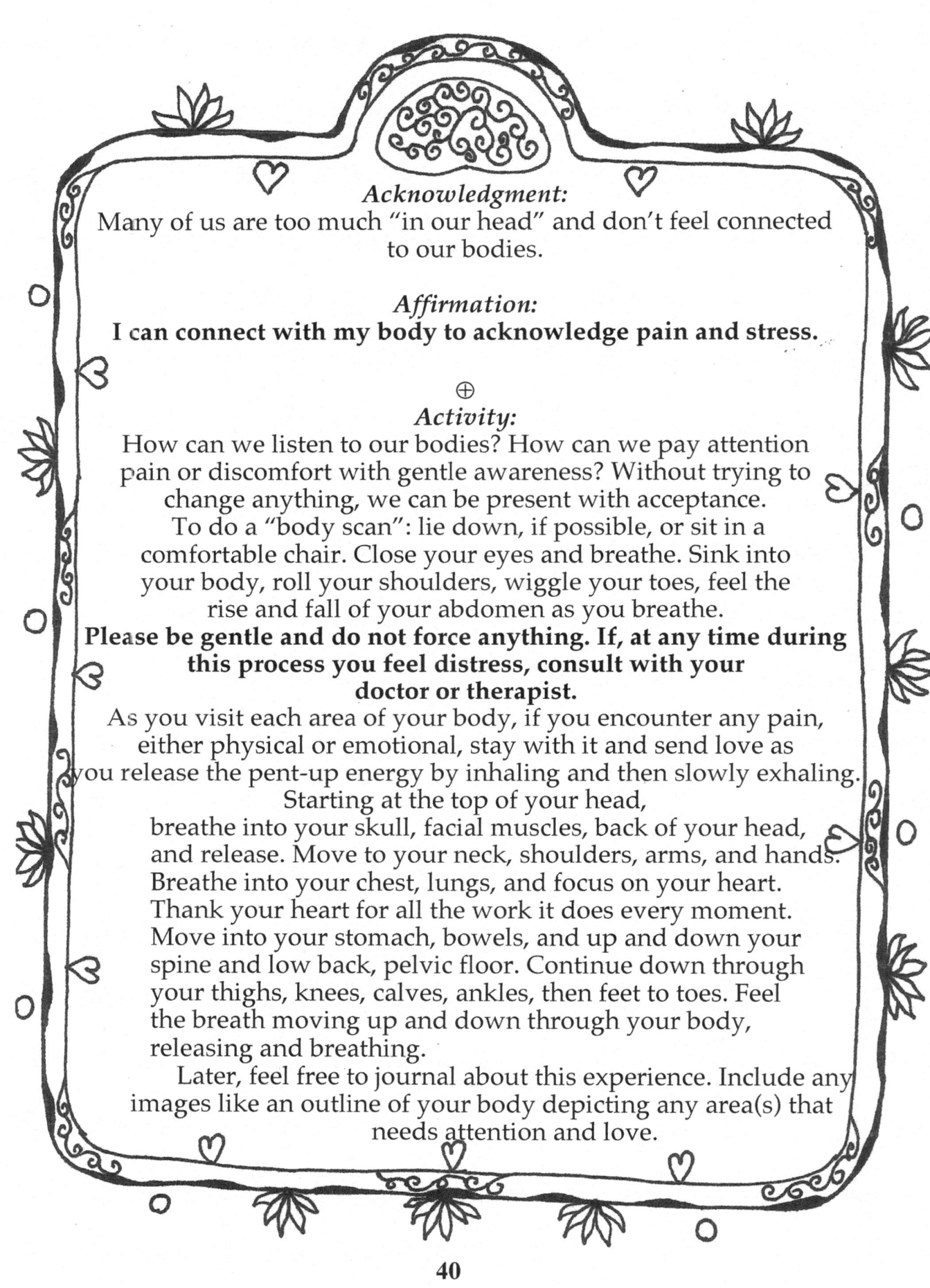

Acknowledgment:
Many of us are too much "in our head" and don't feel connected to our bodies.

Affirmation:
I can connect with my body to acknowledge pain and stress.

⊕

Activity:
How can we listen to our bodies? How can we pay attention pain or discomfort with gentle awareness? Without trying to change anything, we can be present with acceptance.
To do a "body scan": lie down, if possible, or sit in a comfortable chair. Close your eyes and breathe. Sink into your body, roll your shoulders, wiggle your toes, feel the rise and fall of your abdomen as you breathe.
Please be gentle and do not force anything. If, at any time during this process you feel distress, consult with your doctor or therapist.
As you visit each area of your body, if you encounter any pain, either physical or emotional, stay with it and send love as you release the pent-up energy by inhaling and then slowly exhaling. Starting at the top of your head, breathe into your skull, facial muscles, back of your head, and release. Move to your neck, shoulders, arms, and hands. Breathe into your chest, lungs, and focus on your heart. Thank your heart for all the work it does every moment. Move into your stomach, bowels, and up and down your spine and low back, pelvic floor. Continue down through your thighs, knees, calves, ankles, then feet to toes. Feel the breath moving up and down through your body, releasing and breathing.
Later, feel free to journal about this experience. Include any images like an outline of your body depicting any area(s) that needs attention and love.

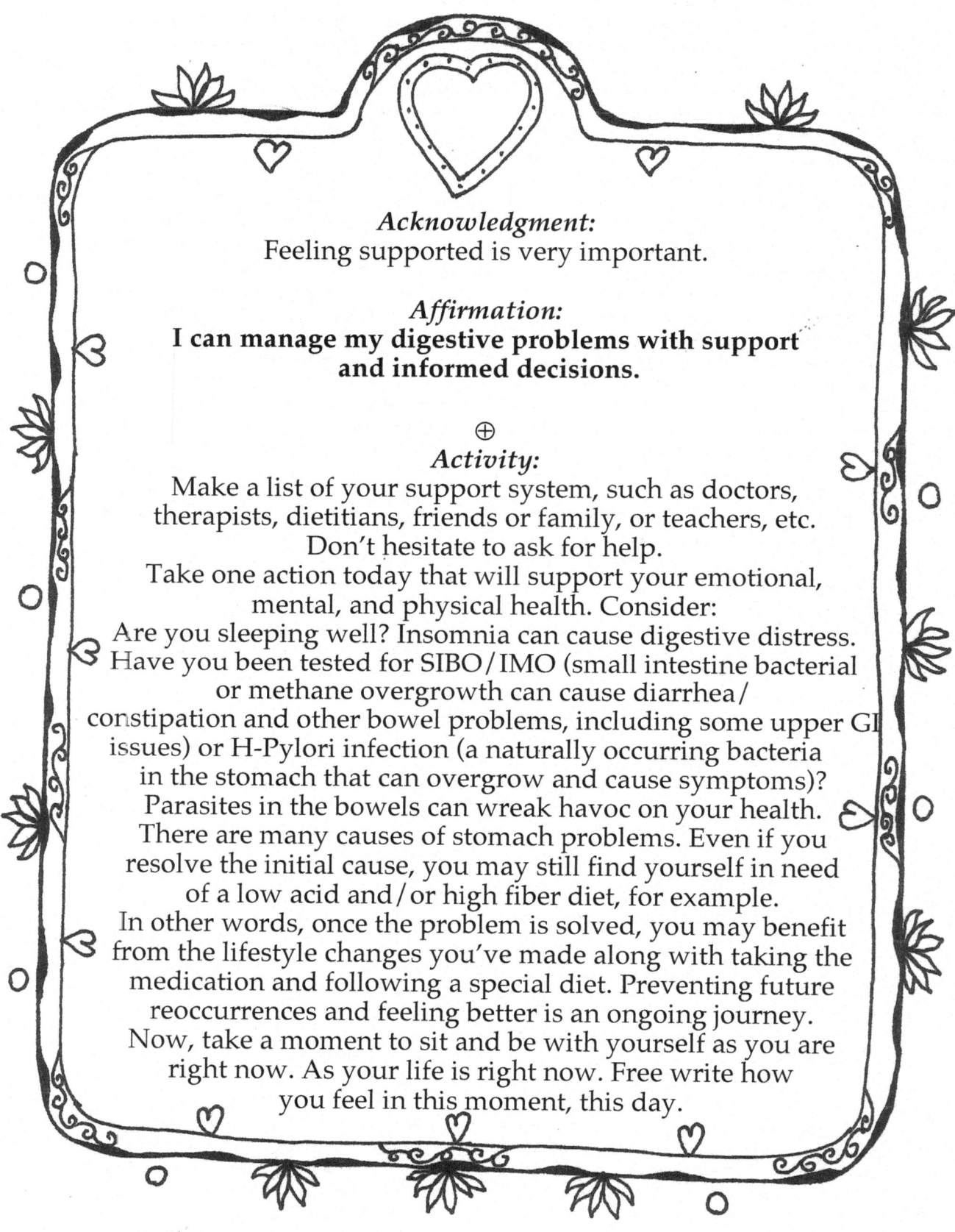

Acknowledgment:
Feeling supported is very important.

Affirmation:
**I can manage my digestive problems with support
and informed decisions.**

⊕

Activity:
Make a list of your support system, such as doctors,
therapists, dietitians, friends or family, or teachers, etc.
Don't hesitate to ask for help.
Take one action today that will support your emotional,
mental, and physical health. Consider:
Are you sleeping well? Insomnia can cause digestive distress.
Have you been tested for SIBO/IMO (small intestine bacterial
or methane overgrowth can cause diarrhea/
constipation and other bowel problems, including some upper GI
issues) or H-Pylori infection (a naturally occurring bacteria
in the stomach that can overgrow and cause symptoms)?
Parasites in the bowels can wreak havoc on your health.
There are many causes of stomach problems. Even if you
resolve the initial cause, you may still find yourself in need
of a low acid and/or high fiber diet, for example.
In other words, once the problem is solved, you may benefit
from the lifestyle changes you've made along with taking the
medication and following a special diet. Preventing future
reoccurrences and feeling better is an ongoing journey.
Now, take a moment to sit and be with yourself as you are
right now. As your life is right now. Free write how
you feel in this moment, this day.

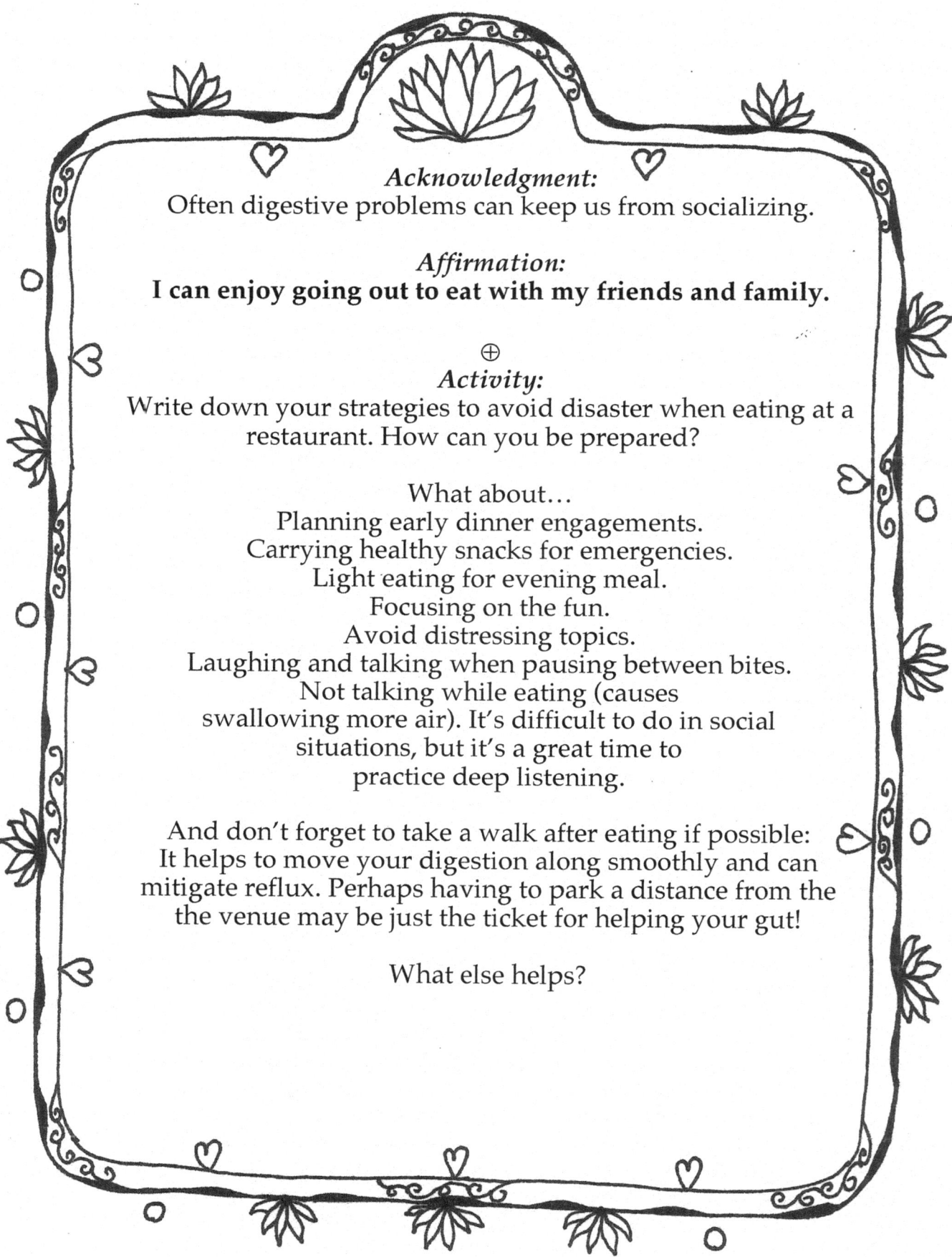

Acknowledgment:
Often digestive problems can keep us from socializing.

Affirmation:
I can enjoy going out to eat with my friends and family.

⊕

Activity:
Write down your strategies to avoid disaster when eating at a restaurant. How can you be prepared?

What about...
Planning early dinner engagements.
Carrying healthy snacks for emergencies.
Light eating for evening meal.
Focusing on the fun.
Avoid distressing topics.
Laughing and talking when pausing between bites.
Not talking while eating (causes
swallowing more air). It's difficult to do in social
situations, but it's a great time to
practice deep listening.

And don't forget to take a walk after eating if possible:
It helps to move your digestion along smoothly and can
mitigate reflux. Perhaps having to park a distance from the
the venue may be just the ticket for helping your gut!

What else helps?

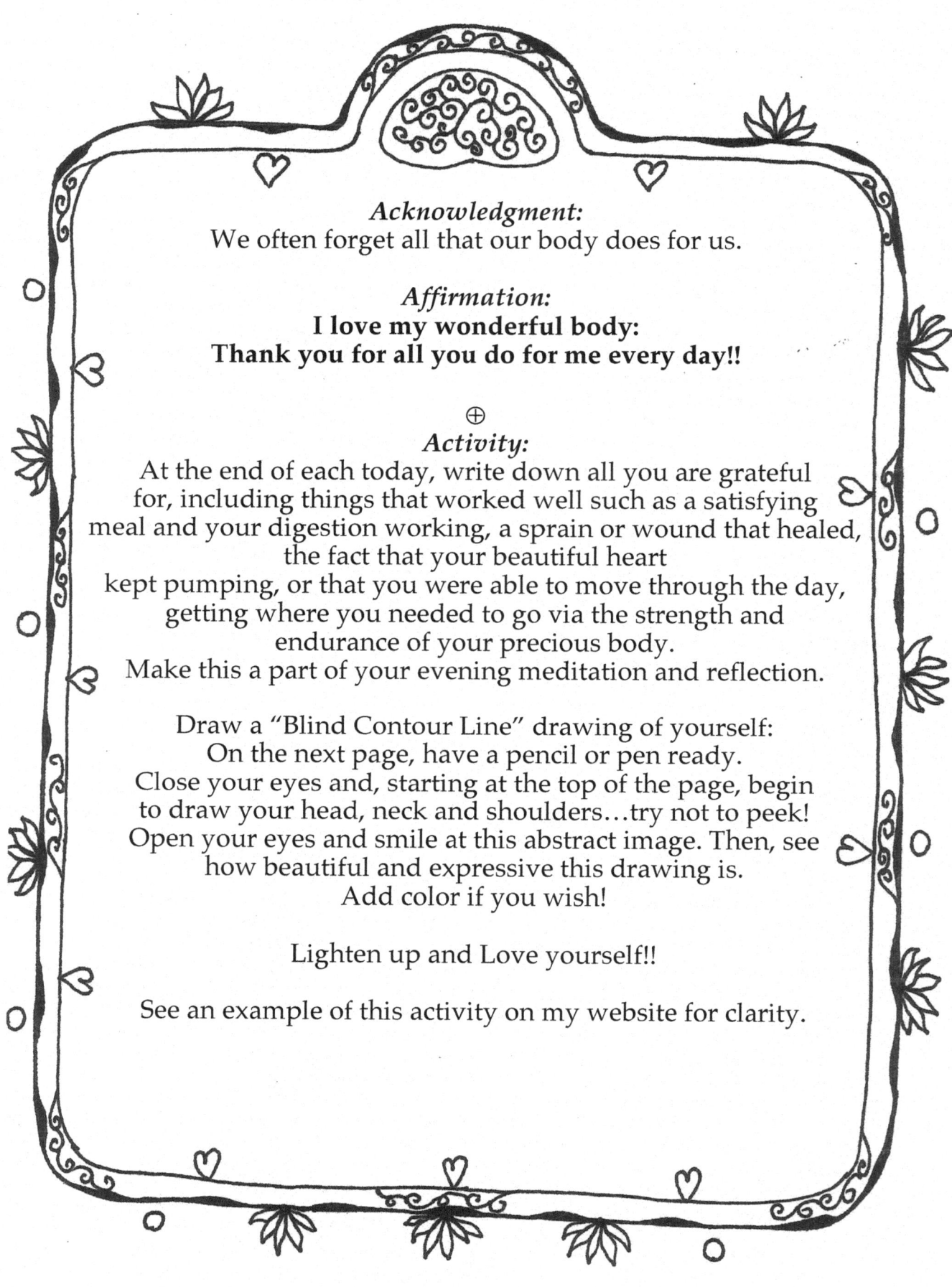

Acknowledgment:
We often forget all that our body does for us.

Affirmation:
I love my wonderful body:
Thank you for all you do for me every day!!

⊕
Activity:
At the end of each today, write down all you are grateful
for, including things that worked well such as a satisfying
meal and your digestion working, a sprain or wound that healed,
the fact that your beautiful heart
kept pumping, or that you were able to move through the day,
getting where you needed to go via the strength and
endurance of your precious body.
Make this a part of your evening meditation and reflection.

Draw a "Blind Contour Line" drawing of yourself:
On the next page, have a pencil or pen ready.
Close your eyes and, starting at the top of the page, begin
to draw your head, neck and shoulders…try not to peek!
Open your eyes and smile at this abstract image. Then, see
how beautiful and expressive this drawing is.
Add color if you wish!

Lighten up and Love yourself!!

See an example of this activity on my website for clarity.

46

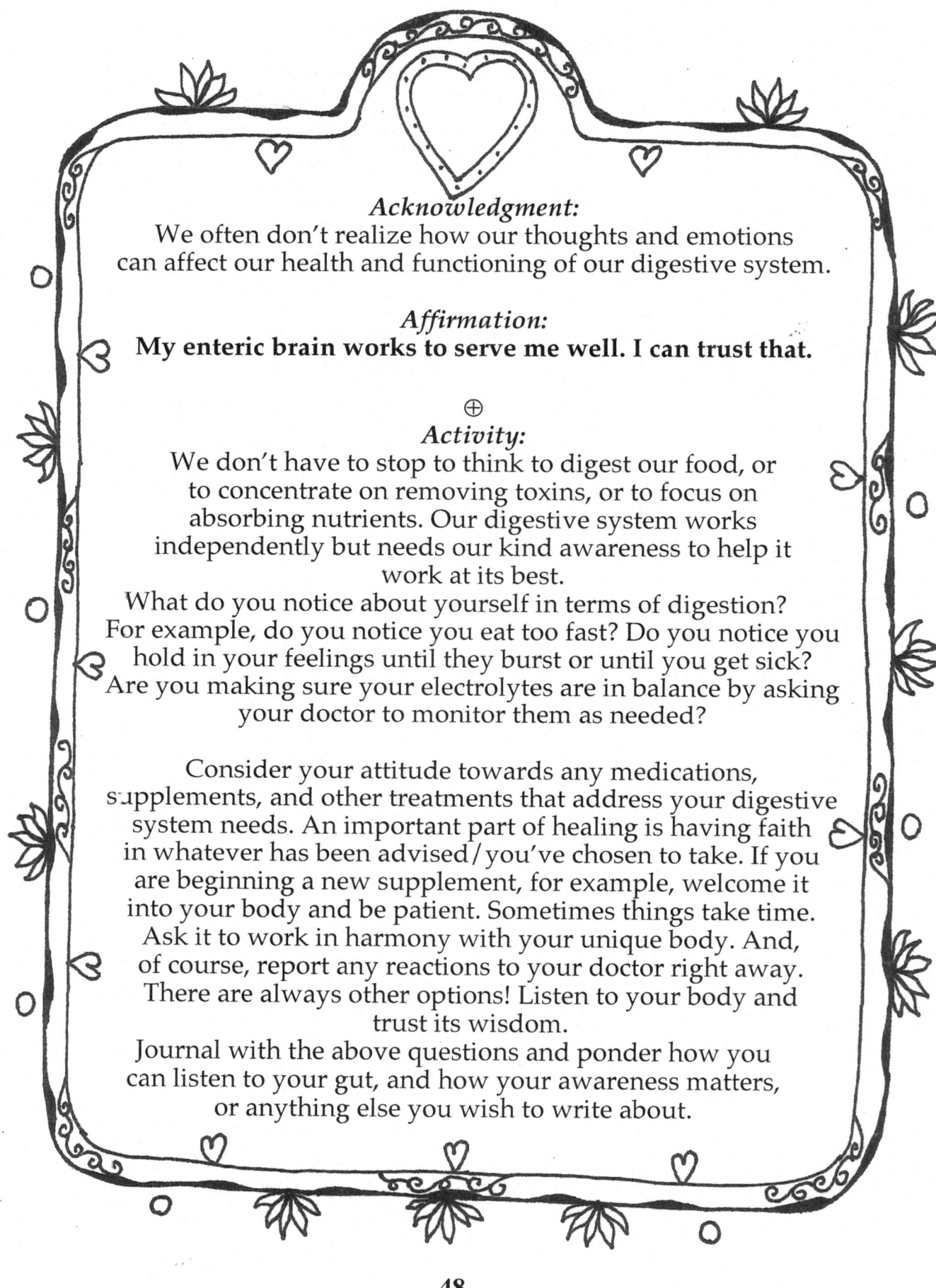

Acknowledgment:
We often don't realize how our thoughts and emotions can affect our health and functioning of our digestive system.

Affirmation:
My enteric brain works to serve me well. I can trust that.

⊕

Activity:
We don't have to stop to think to digest our food, or to concentrate on removing toxins, or to focus on absorbing nutrients. Our digestive system works independently but needs our kind awareness to help it work at its best.
What do you notice about yourself in terms of digestion? For example, do you notice you eat too fast? Do you notice you hold in your feelings until they burst or until you get sick? Are you making sure your electrolytes are in balance by asking your doctor to monitor them as needed?

Consider your attitude towards any medications, supplements, and other treatments that address your digestive system needs. An important part of healing is having faith in whatever has been advised/you've chosen to take. If you are beginning a new supplement, for example, welcome it into your body and be patient. Sometimes things take time. Ask it to work in harmony with your unique body. And, of course, report any reactions to your doctor right away. There are always other options! Listen to your body and trust its wisdom.
Journal with the above questions and ponder how you can listen to your gut, and how your awareness matters, or anything else you wish to write about.

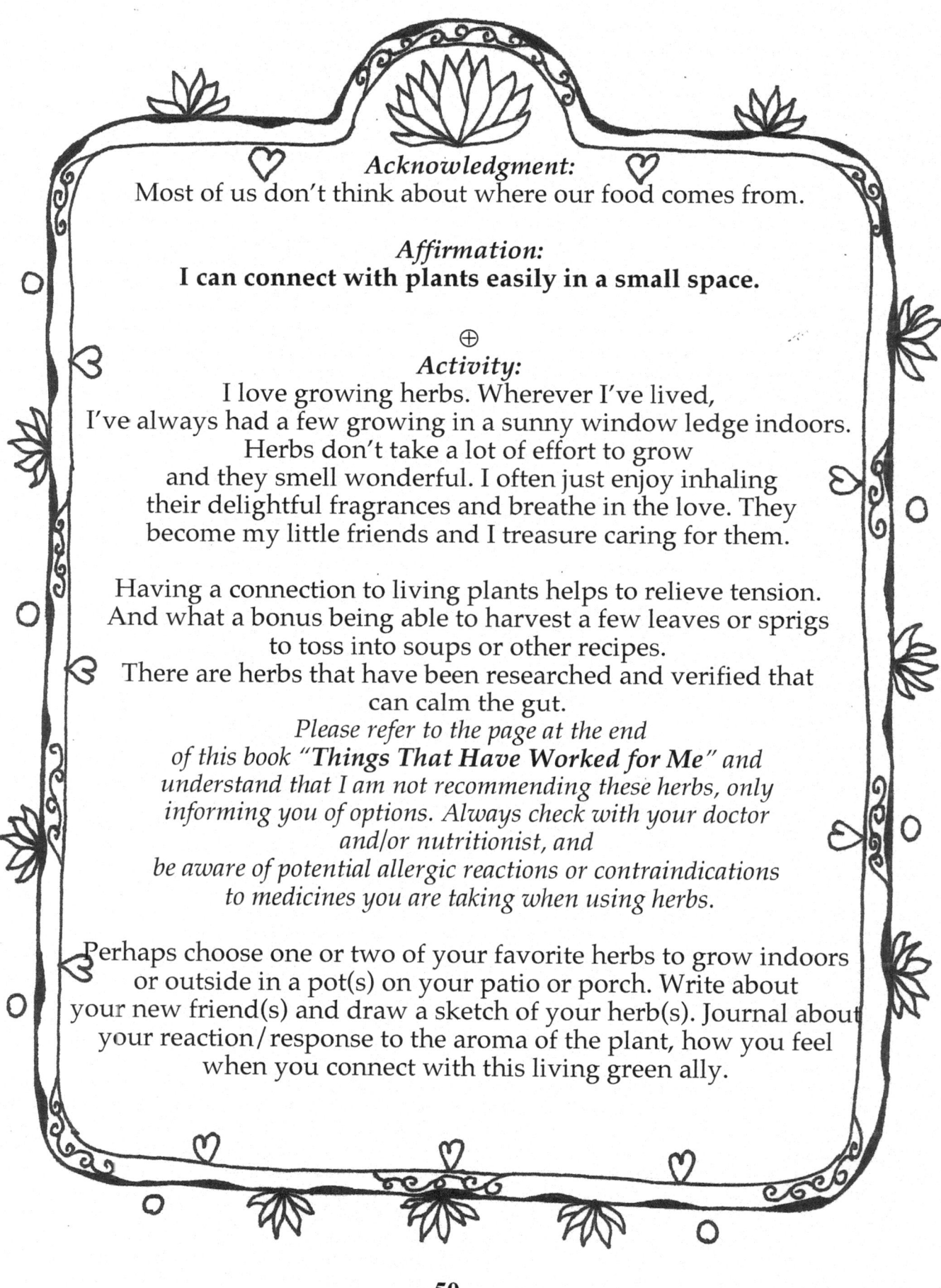

Acknowledgment:
Most of us don't think about where our food comes from.

Affirmation:
I can connect with plants easily in a small space.

⊕
Activity:
I love growing herbs. Wherever I've lived,
I've always had a few growing in a sunny window ledge indoors.
Herbs don't take a lot of effort to grow
and they smell wonderful. I often just enjoy inhaling
their delightful fragrances and breathe in the love. They
become my little friends and I treasure caring for them.

Having a connection to living plants helps to relieve tension.
And what a bonus being able to harvest a few leaves or sprigs
to toss into soups or other recipes.
There are herbs that have been researched and verified that
can calm the gut.
Please refer to the page at the end
*of this book **"Things That Have Worked for Me"** and*
understand that I am not recommending these herbs, only
informing you of options. Always check with your doctor
and/or nutritionist, and
be aware of potential allergic reactions or contraindications
to medicines you are taking when using herbs.

Perhaps choose one or two of your favorite herbs to grow indoors
or outside in a pot(s) on your patio or porch. Write about
your new friend(s) and draw a sketch of your herb(s). Journal about
your reaction/response to the aroma of the plant, how you feel
when you connect with this living green ally.

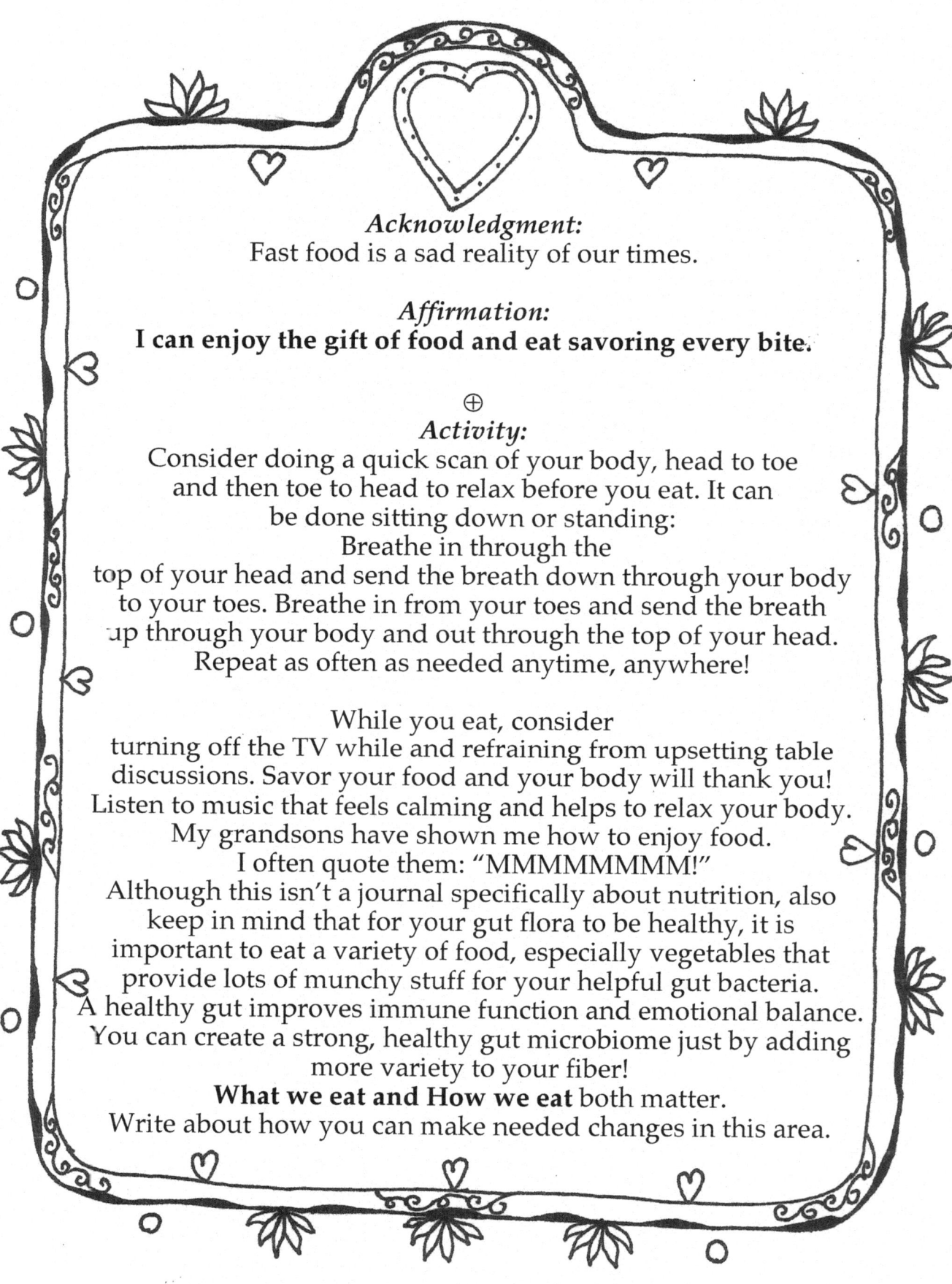

Acknowledgment:
Fast food is a sad reality of our times.

Affirmation:
I can enjoy the gift of food and eat savoring every bite.

⊕

Activity:
Consider doing a quick scan of your body, head to toe
and then toe to head to relax before you eat. It can
be done sitting down or standing:
Breathe in through the
top of your head and send the breath down through your body
to your toes. Breathe in from your toes and send the breath
up through your body and out through the top of your head.
Repeat as often as needed anytime, anywhere!

While you eat, consider
turning off the TV while and refraining from upsetting table
discussions. Savor your food and your body will thank you!
Listen to music that feels calming and helps to relax your body.
My grandsons have shown me how to enjoy food.
I often quote them: "MMMMMMMM!"
Although this isn't a journal specifically about nutrition, also
keep in mind that for your gut flora to be healthy, it is
important to eat a variety of food, especially vegetables that
provide lots of munchy stuff for your helpful gut bacteria.
A healthy gut improves immune function and emotional balance.
You can create a strong, healthy gut microbiome just by adding
more variety to your fiber!
What we eat and How we eat both matter.
Write about how you can make needed changes in this area.

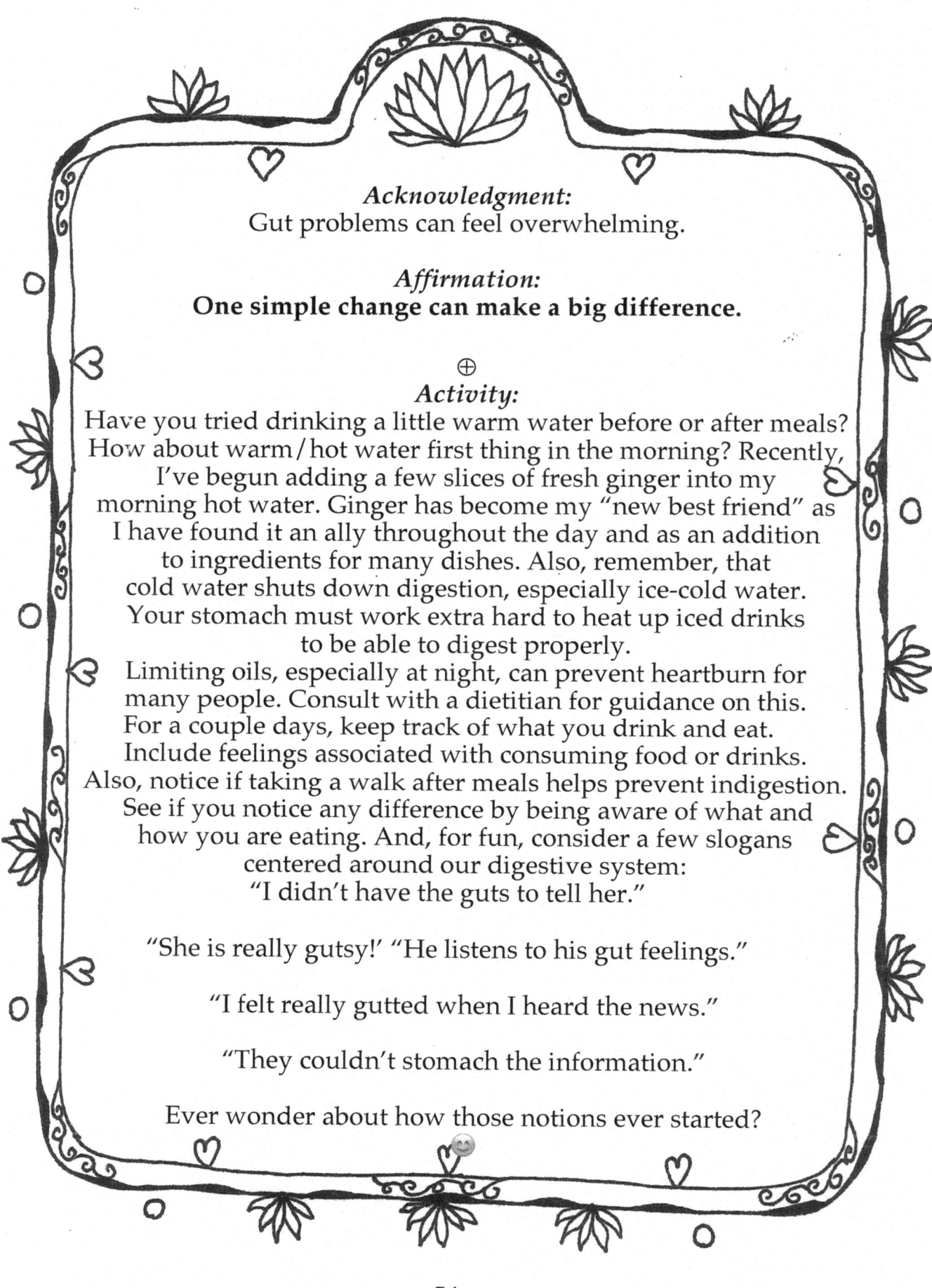

Acknowledgment:
Gut problems can feel overwhelming.

Affirmation:
One simple change can make a big difference.

⊕

Activity:
Have you tried drinking a little warm water before or after meals?
How about warm/hot water first thing in the morning? Recently,
I've begun adding a few slices of fresh ginger into my
morning hot water. Ginger has become my "new best friend" as
I have found it an ally throughout the day and as an addition
to ingredients for many dishes. Also, remember, that
cold water shuts down digestion, especially ice-cold water.
Your stomach must work extra hard to heat up iced drinks
to be able to digest properly.
Limiting oils, especially at night, can prevent heartburn for
many people. Consult with a dietitian for guidance on this.
For a couple days, keep track of what you drink and eat.
Include feelings associated with consuming food or drinks.
Also, notice if taking a walk after meals helps prevent indigestion.
See if you notice any difference by being aware of what and
how you are eating. And, for fun, consider a few slogans
centered around our digestive system:
"I didn't have the guts to tell her."

"She is really gutsy!' "He listens to his gut feelings."

"I felt really gutted when I heard the news."

"They couldn't stomach the information."

Ever wonder about how those notions ever started?

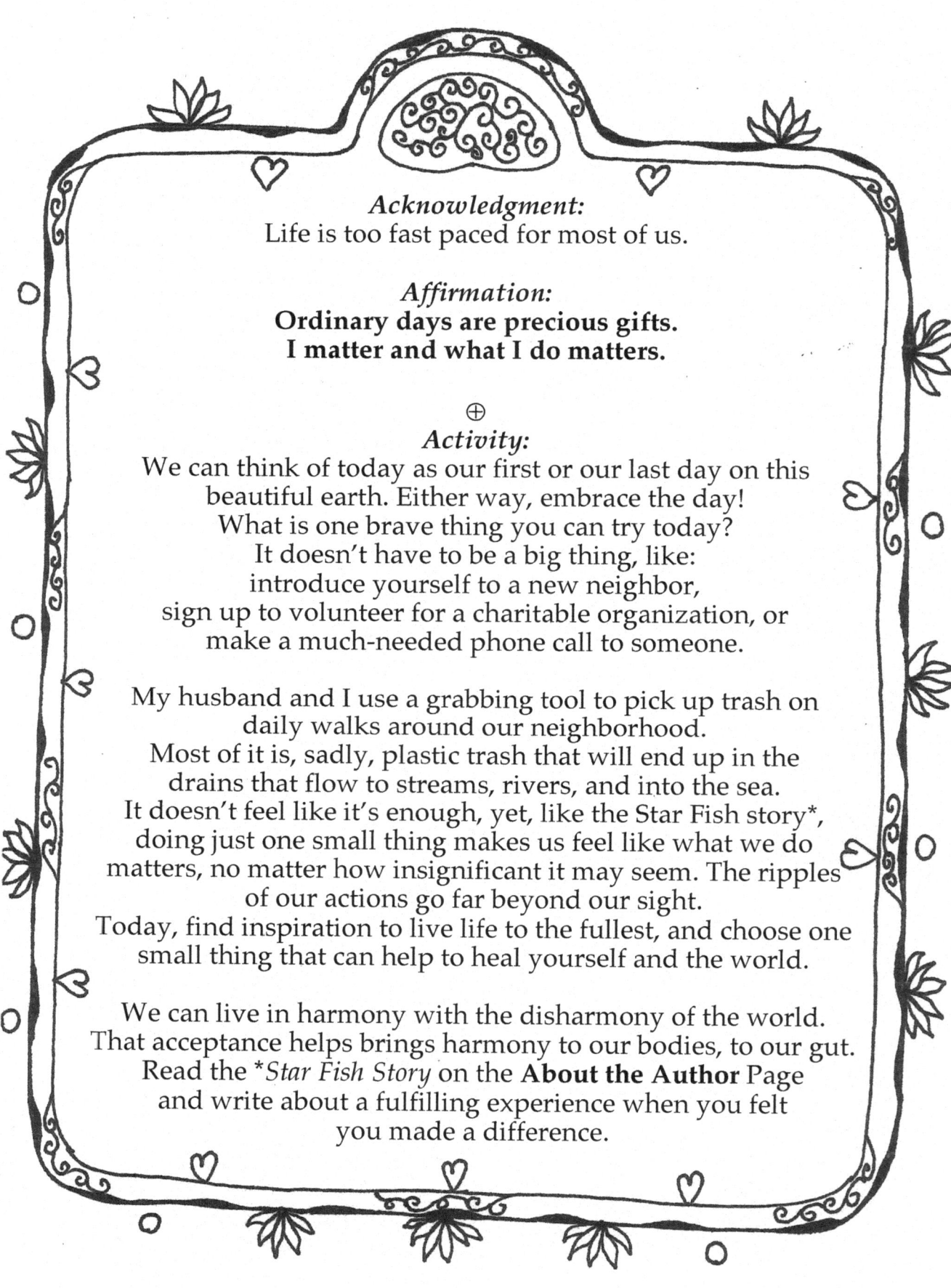

Acknowledgment:
Life is too fast paced for most of us.

Affirmation:
Ordinary days are precious gifts.
I matter and what I do matters.

⊕

Activity:
We can think of today as our first or our last day on this
beautiful earth. Either way, embrace the day!
What is one brave thing you can try today?
It doesn't have to be a big thing, like:
introduce yourself to a new neighbor,
sign up to volunteer for a charitable organization, or
make a much-needed phone call to someone.

My husband and I use a grabbing tool to pick up trash on
daily walks around our neighborhood.
Most of it is, sadly, plastic trash that will end up in the
drains that flow to streams, rivers, and into the sea.
It doesn't feel like it's enough, yet, like the Star Fish story*,
doing just one small thing makes us feel like what we do
matters, no matter how insignificant it may seem. The ripples
of our actions go far beyond our sight.
Today, find inspiration to live life to the fullest, and choose one
small thing that can help to heal yourself and the world.

We can live in harmony with the disharmony of the world.
That acceptance helps brings harmony to our bodies, to our gut.
Read the **Star Fish Story* on the **About the Author** Page
and write about a fulfilling experience when you felt
you made a difference.

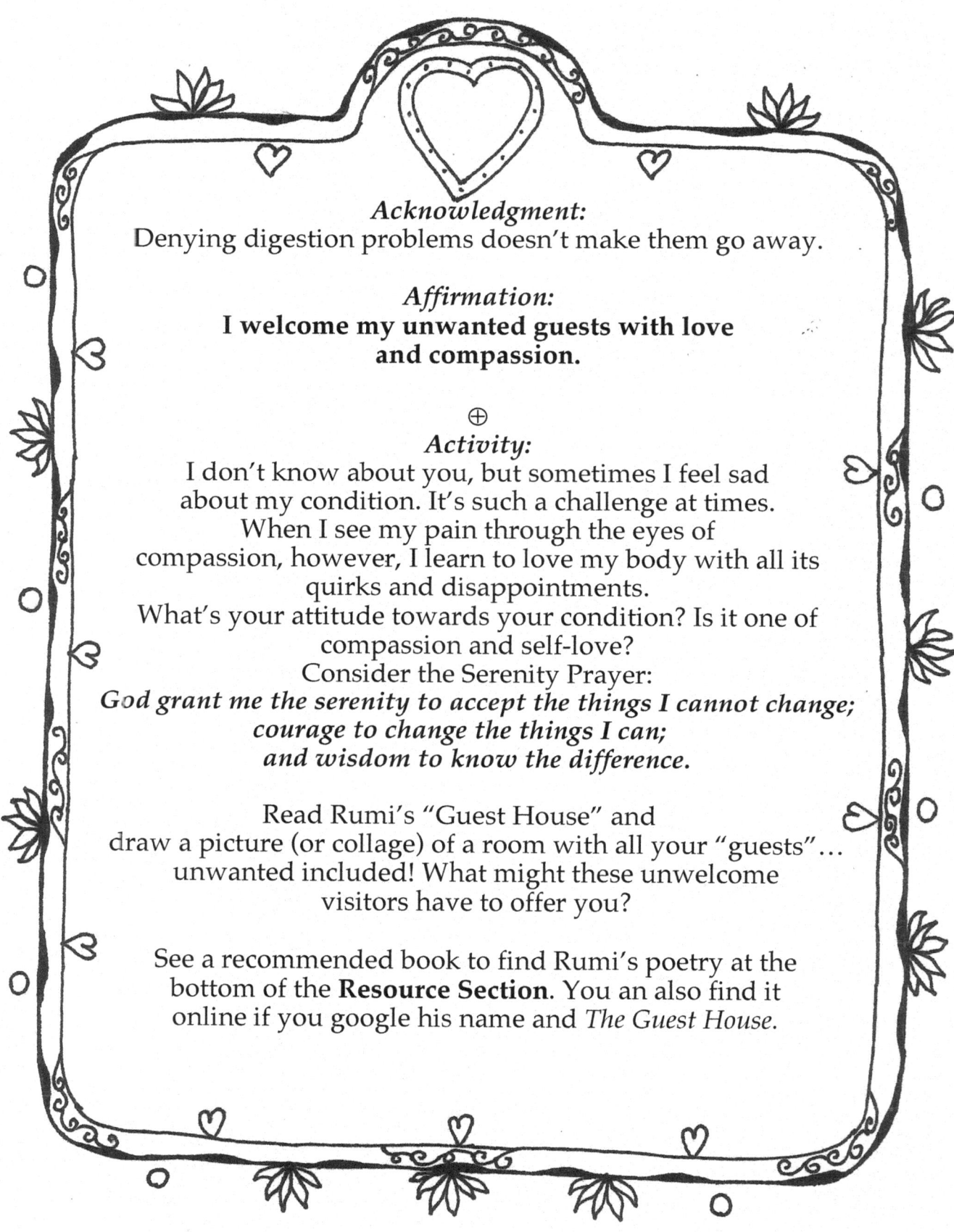

Acknowledgment:
Denying digestion problems doesn't make them go away.

Affirmation:
**I welcome my unwanted guests with love
and compassion.**

⊕
Activity:
I don't know about you, but sometimes I feel sad
about my condition. It's such a challenge at times.
When I see my pain through the eyes of
compassion, however, I learn to love my body with all its
quirks and disappointments.
What's your attitude towards your condition? Is it one of
compassion and self-love?
Consider the Serenity Prayer:
God grant me the serenity to accept the things I cannot change;
courage to change the things I can;
and wisdom to know the difference.

Read Rumi's "Guest House" and
draw a picture (or collage) of a room with all your "guests"…
unwanted included! What might these unwelcome
visitors have to offer you?

See a recommended book to find Rumi's poetry at the
bottom of the **Resource Section**. You an also find it
online if you google his name and *The Guest House.*

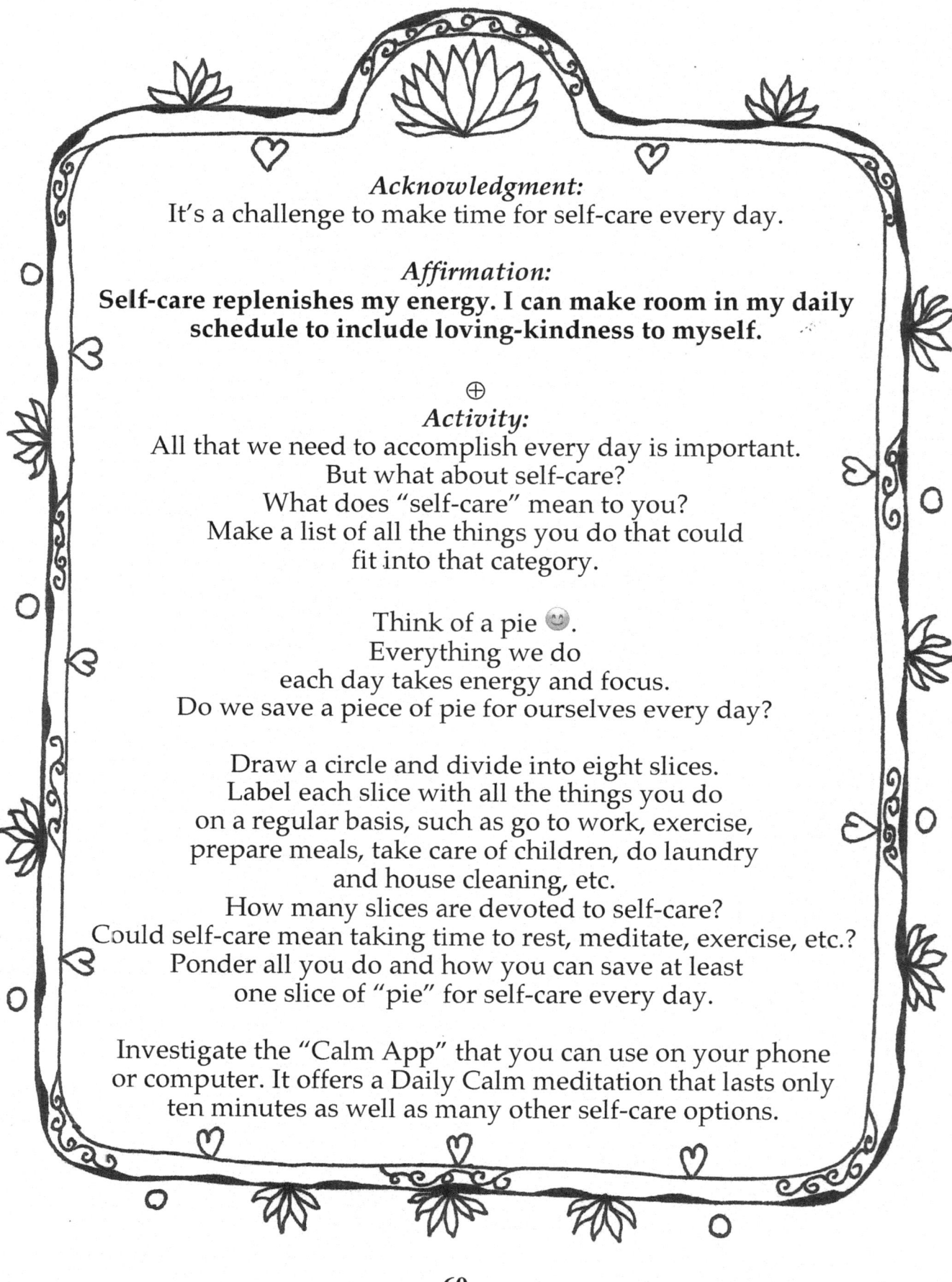

Acknowledgment:
It's a challenge to make time for self-care every day.

Affirmation:
Self-care replenishes my energy. I can make room in my daily schedule to include loving-kindness to myself.

⊕

Activity:
All that we need to accomplish every day is important.
But what about self-care?
What does "self-care" mean to you?
Make a list of all the things you do that could
fit into that category.

Think of a pie 😊.
Everything we do
each day takes energy and focus.
Do we save a piece of pie for ourselves every day?

Draw a circle and divide into eight slices.
Label each slice with all the things you do
on a regular basis, such as go to work, exercise,
prepare meals, take care of children, do laundry
and house cleaning, etc.
How many slices are devoted to self-care?
Could self-care mean taking time to rest, meditate, exercise, etc.?
Ponder all you do and how you can save at least
one slice of "pie" for self-care every day.

Investigate the "Calm App" that you can use on your phone
or computer. It offers a Daily Calm meditation that lasts only
ten minutes as well as many other self-care options.

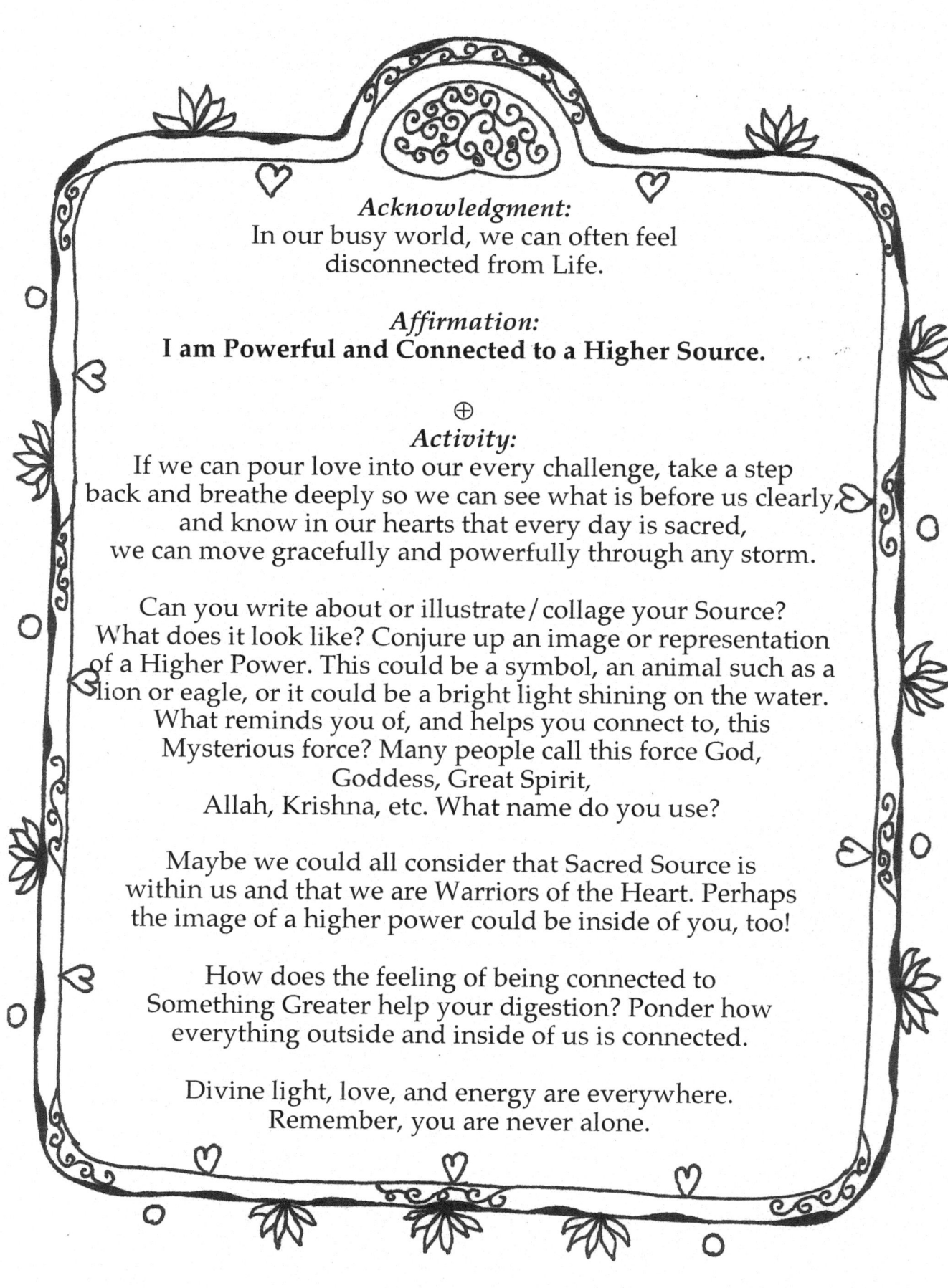

Acknowledgment:
In our busy world, we can often feel
disconnected from Life.

Affirmation:
I am Powerful and Connected to a Higher Source.

⊕

Activity:
If we can pour love into our every challenge, take a step
back and breathe deeply so we can see what is before us clearly,
and know in our hearts that every day is sacred,
we can move gracefully and powerfully through any storm.

Can you write about or illustrate/collage your Source?
What does it look like? Conjure up an image or representation
of a Higher Power. This could be a symbol, an animal such as a
lion or eagle, or it could be a bright light shining on the water.
What reminds you of, and helps you connect to, this
Mysterious force? Many people call this force God,
Goddess, Great Spirit,
Allah, Krishna, etc. What name do you use?

Maybe we could all consider that Sacred Source is
within us and that we are Warriors of the Heart. Perhaps
the image of a higher power could be inside of you, too!

How does the feeling of being connected to
Something Greater help your digestion? Ponder how
everything outside and inside of us is connected.

Divine light, love, and energy are everywhere.
Remember, you are never alone.

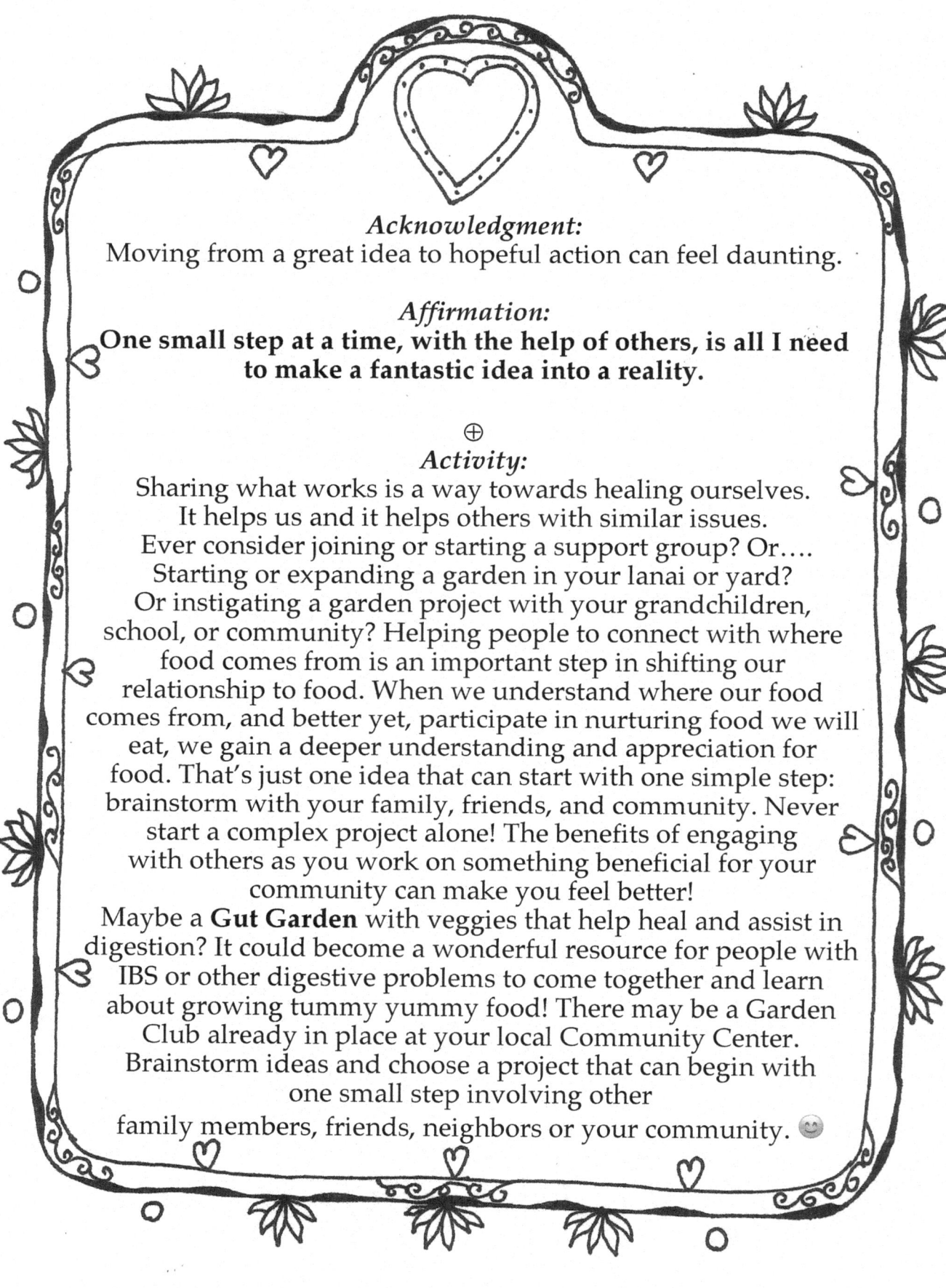

Acknowledgment:
Moving from a great idea to hopeful action can feel daunting.

Affirmation:
**One small step at a time, with the help of others, is all I need
to make a fantastic idea into a reality.**

⊕

Activity:
Sharing what works is a way towards healing ourselves.
It helps us and it helps others with similar issues.
Ever consider joining or starting a support group? Or....
Starting or expanding a garden in your lanai or yard?
Or instigating a garden project with your grandchildren,
school, or community? Helping people to connect with where
food comes from is an important step in shifting our
relationship to food. When we understand where our food
comes from, and better yet, participate in nurturing food we will
eat, we gain a deeper understanding and appreciation for
food. That's just one idea that can start with one simple step:
brainstorm with your family, friends, and community. Never
start a complex project alone! The benefits of engaging
with others as you work on something beneficial for your
community can make you feel better!
Maybe a **Gut Garden** with veggies that help heal and assist in
digestion? It could become a wonderful resource for people with
IBS or other digestive problems to come together and learn
about growing tummy yummy food! There may be a Garden
Club already in place at your local Community Center.
Brainstorm ideas and choose a project that can begin with
one small step involving other
family members, friends, neighbors or your community. 😊

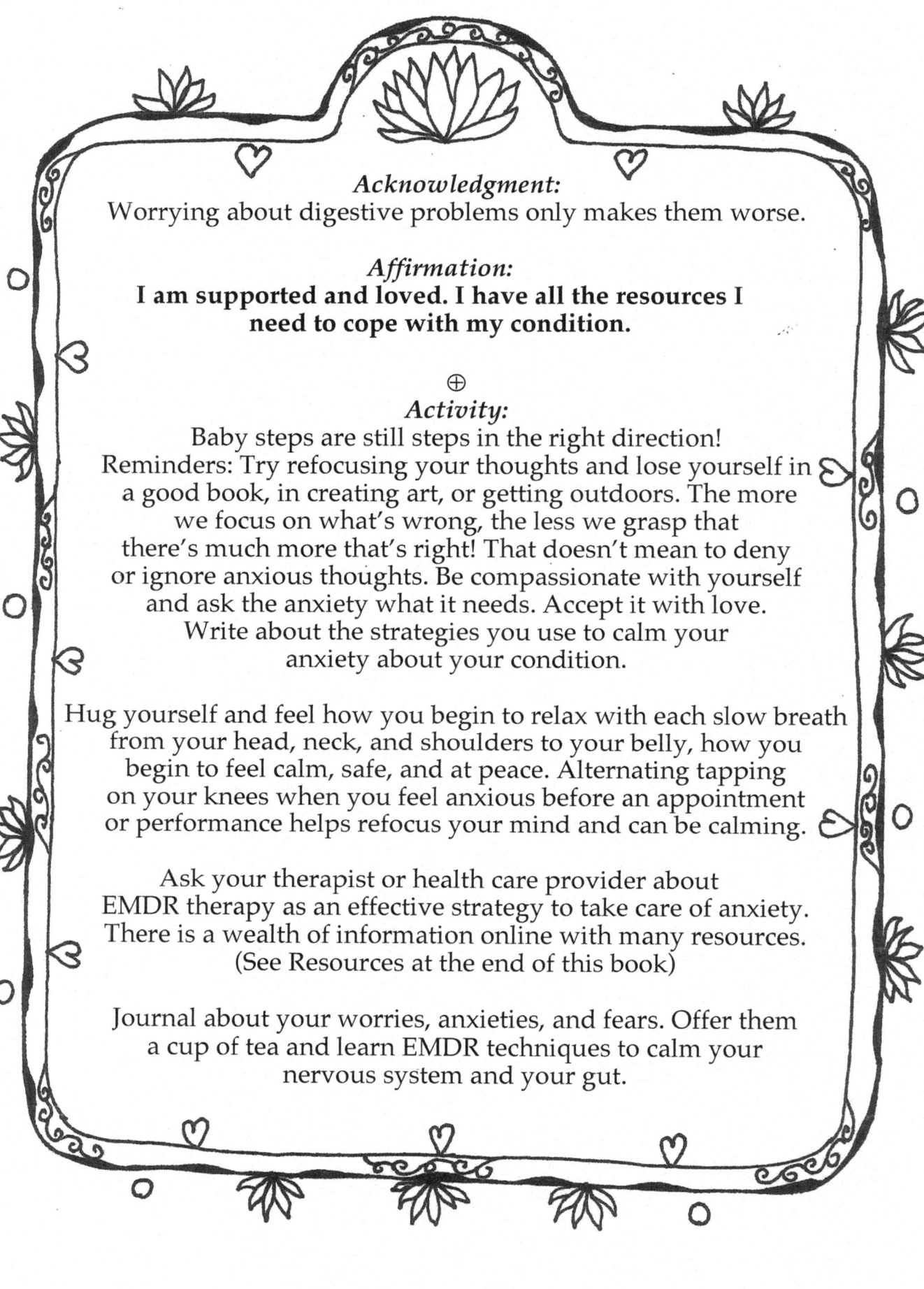

Acknowledgment:
Worrying about digestive problems only makes them worse.

Affirmation:
**I am supported and loved. I have all the resources I
need to cope with my condition.**

⊕

Activity:
Baby steps are still steps in the right direction!
Reminders: Try refocusing your thoughts and lose yourself in
a good book, in creating art, or getting outdoors. The more
we focus on what's wrong, the less we grasp that
there's much more that's right! That doesn't mean to deny
or ignore anxious thoughts. Be compassionate with yourself
and ask the anxiety what it needs. Accept it with love.
Write about the strategies you use to calm your
anxiety about your condition.

Hug yourself and feel how you begin to relax with each slow breath
from your head, neck, and shoulders to your belly, how you
begin to feel calm, safe, and at peace. Alternating tapping
on your knees when you feel anxious before an appointment
or performance helps refocus your mind and can be calming.

Ask your therapist or health care provider about
EMDR therapy as an effective strategy to take care of anxiety.
There is a wealth of information online with many resources.
(See Resources at the end of this book)

Journal about your worries, anxieties, and fears. Offer them
a cup of tea and learn EMDR techniques to calm your
nervous system and your gut.

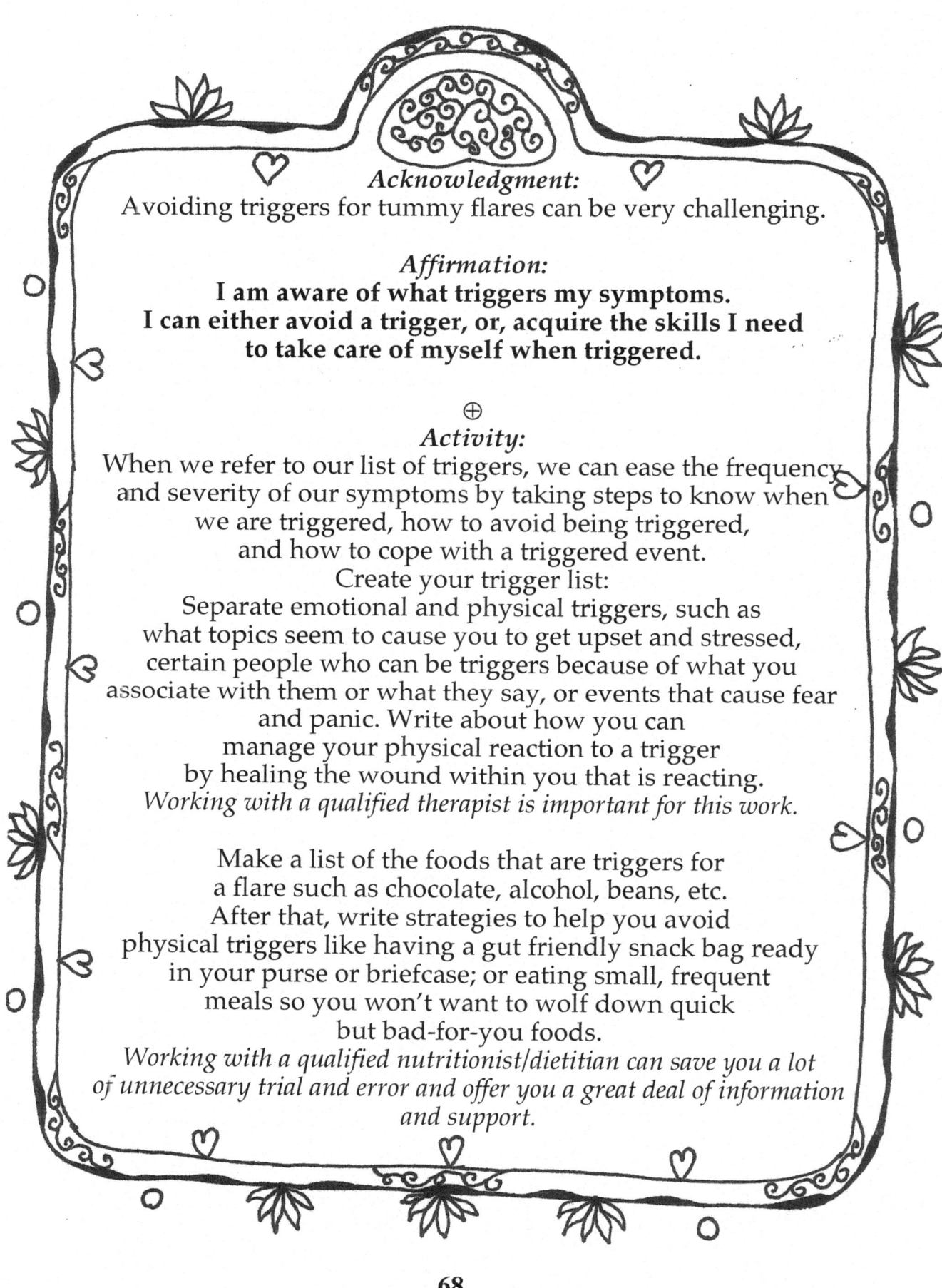

Acknowledgment:
Avoiding triggers for tummy flares can be very challenging.

Affirmation:
I am aware of what triggers my symptoms.
I can either avoid a trigger, or, acquire the skills I need
to take care of myself when triggered.

⊕

Activity:
When we refer to our list of triggers, we can ease the frequency
and severity of our symptoms by taking steps to know when
we are triggered, how to avoid being triggered,
and how to cope with a triggered event.
Create your trigger list:
Separate emotional and physical triggers, such as
what topics seem to cause you to get upset and stressed,
certain people who can be triggers because of what you
associate with them or what they say, or events that cause fear
and panic. Write about how you can
manage your physical reaction to a trigger
by healing the wound within you that is reacting.
Working with a qualified therapist is important for this work.

Make a list of the foods that are triggers for
a flare such as chocolate, alcohol, beans, etc.
After that, write strategies to help you avoid
physical triggers like having a gut friendly snack bag ready
in your purse or briefcase; or eating small, frequent
meals so you won't want to wolf down quick
but bad-for-you foods.
Working with a qualified nutritionist/dietitian can save you a lot
of unnecessary trial and error and offer you a great deal of information
and support.

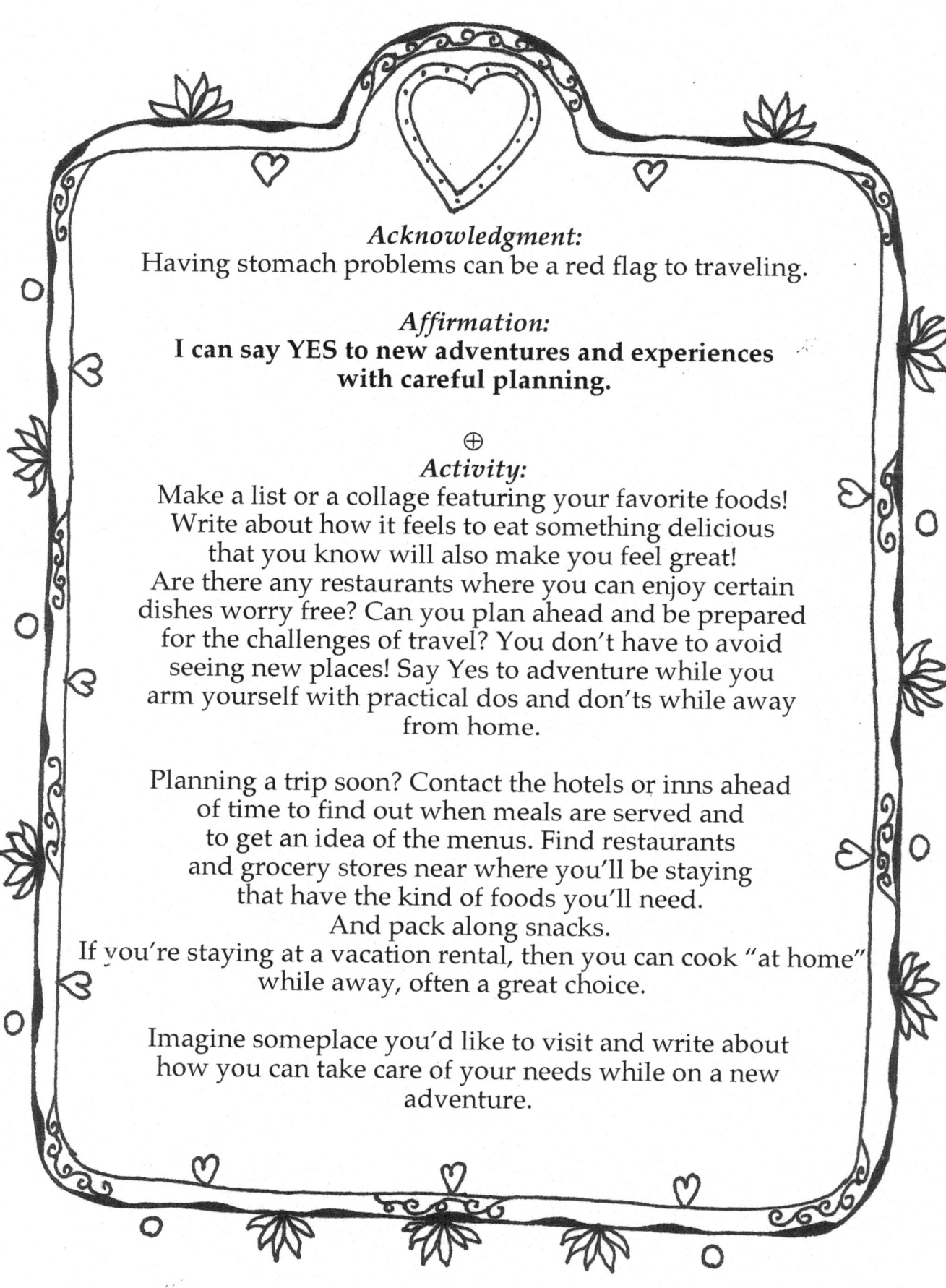

Acknowledgment:
Having stomach problems can be a red flag to traveling.

Affirmation:
**I can say YES to new adventures and experiences
with careful planning.**

⊕

Activity:
Make a list or a collage featuring your favorite foods!
Write about how it feels to eat something delicious
that you know will also make you feel great!
Are there any restaurants where you can enjoy certain
dishes worry free? Can you plan ahead and be prepared
for the challenges of travel? You don't have to avoid
seeing new places! Say Yes to adventure while you
arm yourself with practical dos and don'ts while away
from home.

Planning a trip soon? Contact the hotels or inns ahead
of time to find out when meals are served and
to get an idea of the menus. Find restaurants
and grocery stores near where you'll be staying
that have the kind of foods you'll need.
And pack along snacks.
If you're staying at a vacation rental, then you can cook "at home"
while away, often a great choice.

Imagine someplace you'd like to visit and write about
how you can take care of your needs while on a new
adventure.

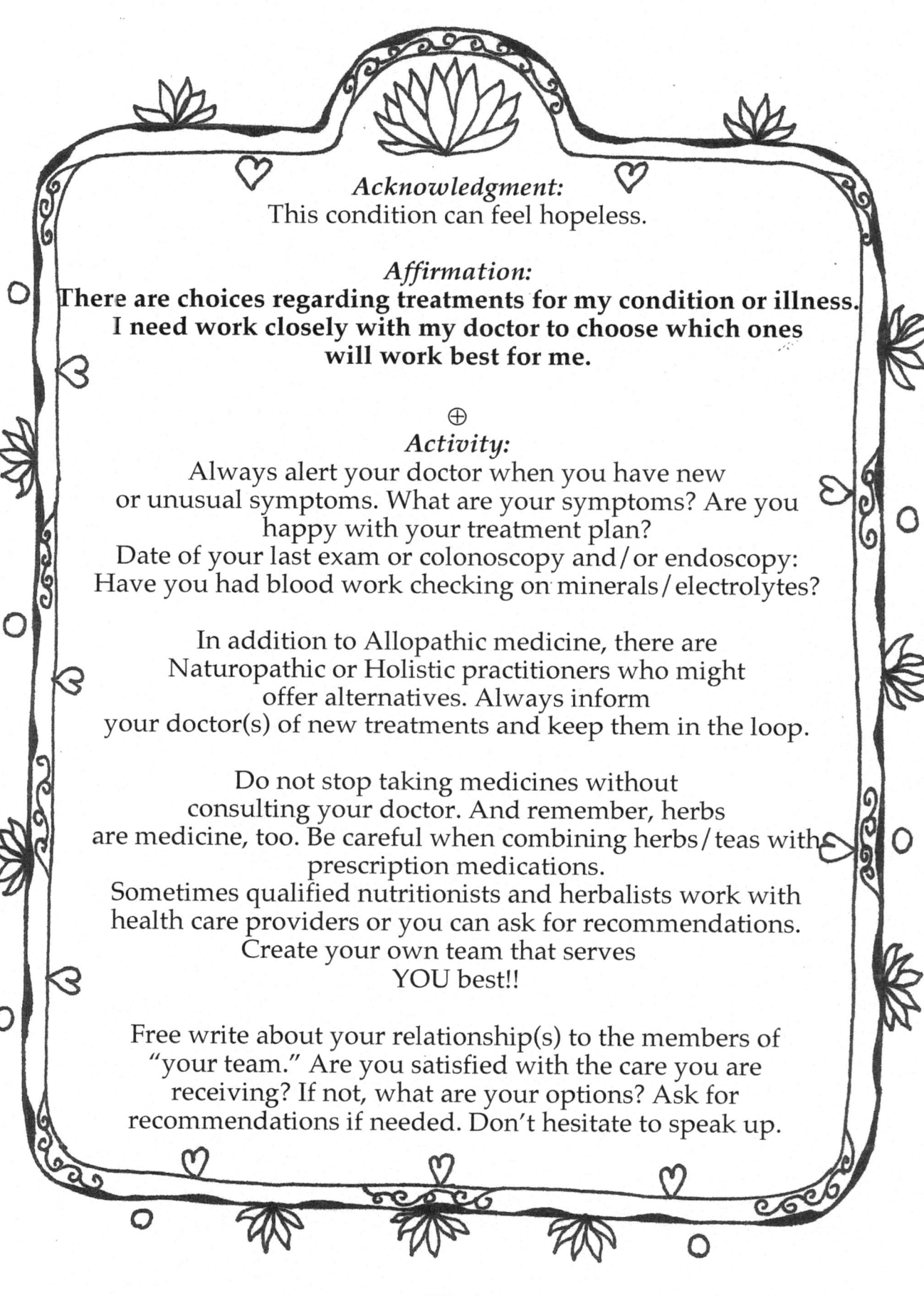

Acknowledgment:
This condition can feel hopeless.

Affirmation:
**There are choices regarding treatments for my condition or illness.
I need work closely with my doctor to choose which ones
will work best for me.**

⊕
Activity:
Always alert your doctor when you have new
or unusual symptoms. What are your symptoms? Are you
happy with your treatment plan?
Date of your last exam or colonoscopy and/or endoscopy:
Have you had blood work checking on minerals/electrolytes?

In addition to Allopathic medicine, there are
Naturopathic or Holistic practitioners who might
offer alternatives. Always inform
your doctor(s) of new treatments and keep them in the loop.

Do not stop taking medicines without
consulting your doctor. And remember, herbs
are medicine, too. Be careful when combining herbs/teas with
prescription medications.
Sometimes qualified nutritionists and herbalists work with
health care providers or you can ask for recommendations.
Create your own team that serves
YOU best!!

Free write about your relationship(s) to the members of
"your team." Are you satisfied with the care you are
receiving? If not, what are your options? Ask for
recommendations if needed. Don't hesitate to speak up.

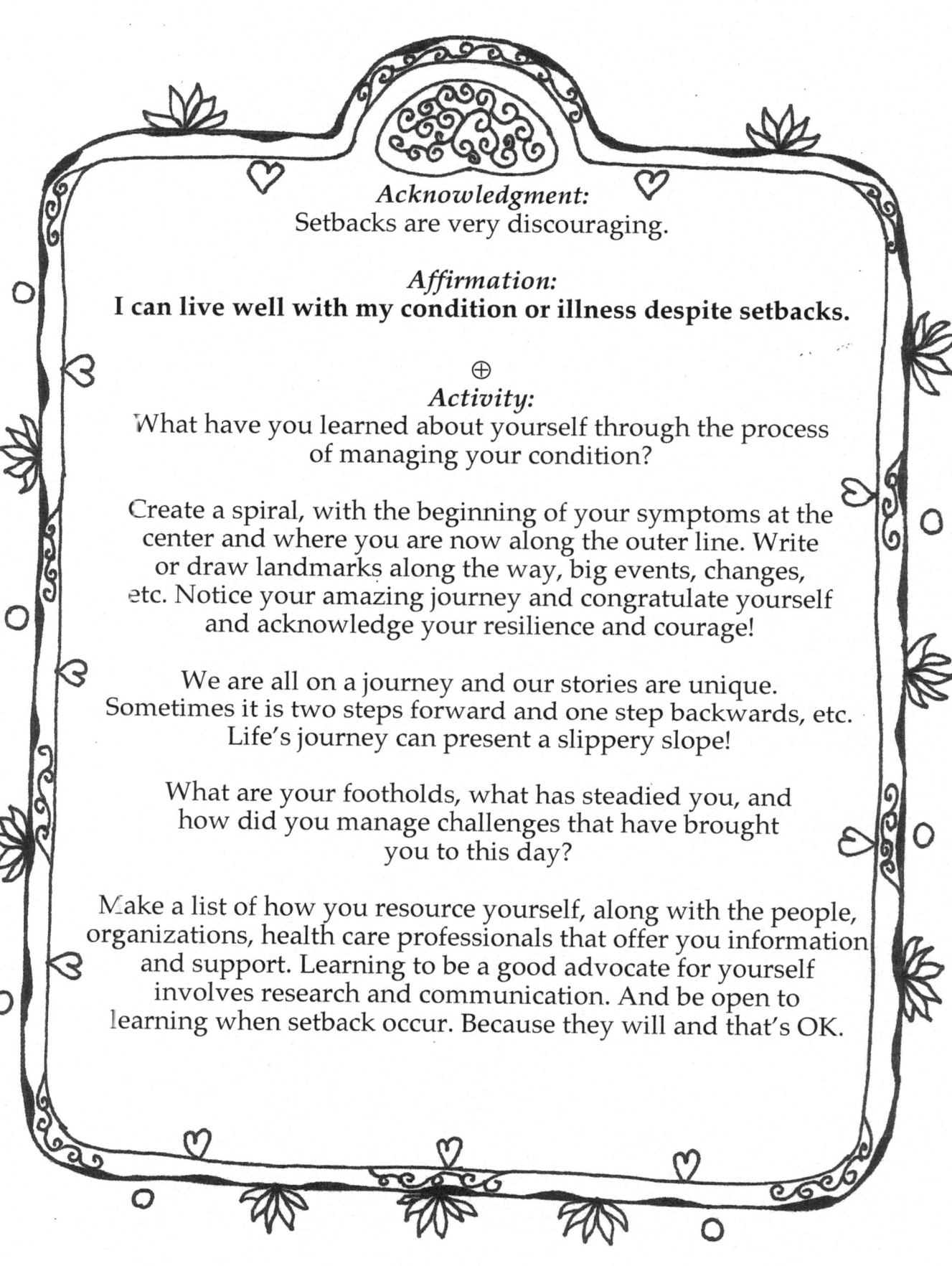

Acknowledgment:
Setbacks are very discouraging.

Affirmation:
I can live well with my condition or illness despite setbacks.

⊕

Activity:
What have you learned about yourself through the process
of managing your condition?

Create a spiral, with the beginning of your symptoms at the
center and where you are now along the outer line. Write
or draw landmarks along the way, big events, changes,
etc. Notice your amazing journey and congratulate yourself
and acknowledge your resilience and courage!

We are all on a journey and our stories are unique.
Sometimes it is two steps forward and one step backwards, etc.
Life's journey can present a slippery slope!

What are your footholds, what has steadied you, and
how did you manage challenges that have brought
you to this day?

Make a list of how you resource yourself, along with the people,
organizations, health care professionals that offer you information
and support. Learning to be a good advocate for yourself
involves research and communication. And be open to
learning when setback occur. Because they will and that's OK.

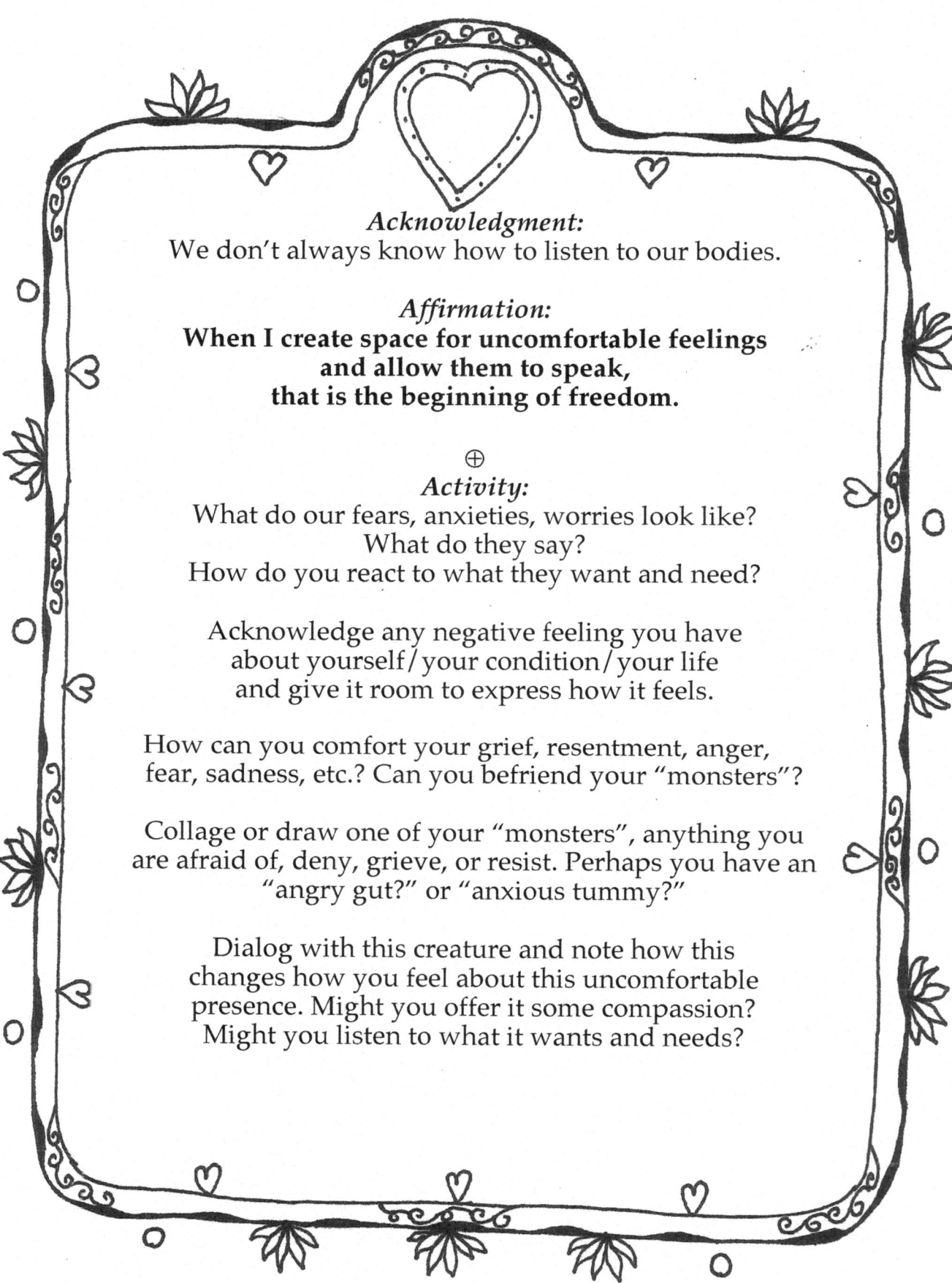

Acknowledgment:
We don't always know how to listen to our bodies.

Affirmation:
**When I create space for uncomfortable feelings
and allow them to speak,
that is the beginning of freedom.**

⊕

Activity:
What do our fears, anxieties, worries look like?
What do they say?
How do you react to what they want and need?

Acknowledge any negative feeling you have
about yourself/your condition/your life
and give it room to express how it feels.

How can you comfort your grief, resentment, anger,
fear, sadness, etc.? Can you befriend your "monsters"?

Collage or draw one of your "monsters", anything you
are afraid of, deny, grieve, or resist. Perhaps you have an
"angry gut?" or "anxious tummy?"

Dialog with this creature and note how this
changes how you feel about this uncomfortable
presence. Might you offer it some compassion?
Might you listen to what it wants and needs?

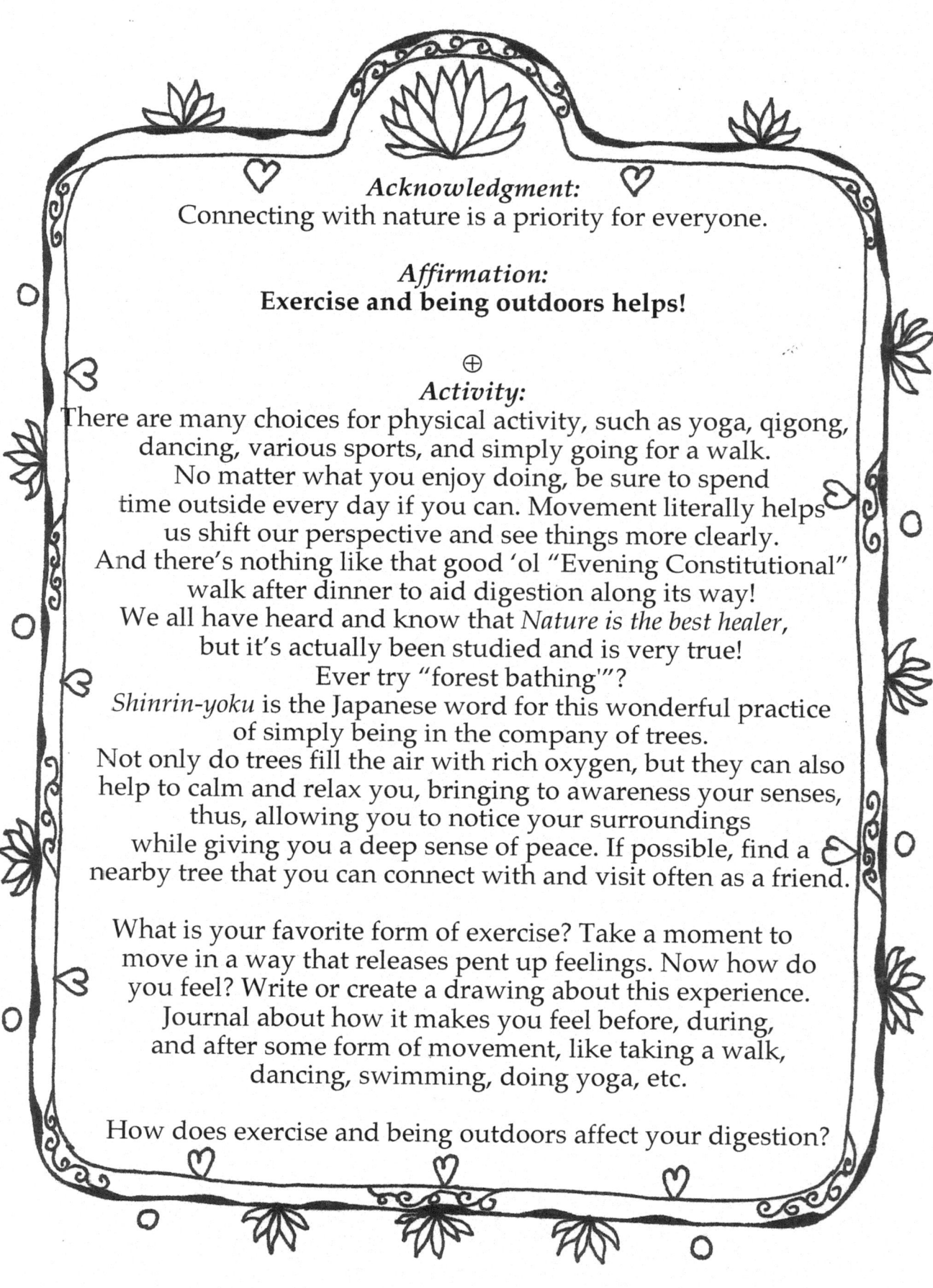

Acknowledgment:
Connecting with nature is a priority for everyone.

Affirmation:
Exercise and being outdoors helps!

⊕

Activity:
There are many choices for physical activity, such as yoga, qigong,
dancing, various sports, and simply going for a walk.
No matter what you enjoy doing, be sure to spend
time outside every day if you can. Movement literally helps
us shift our perspective and see things more clearly.
And there's nothing like that good 'ol "Evening Constitutional"
walk after dinner to aid digestion along its way!
We all have heard and know that *Nature is the best healer*,
but it's actually been studied and is very true!
Ever try "forest bathing'"?
Shinrin-yoku is the Japanese word for this wonderful practice
of simply being in the company of trees.
Not only do trees fill the air with rich oxygen, but they can also
help to calm and relax you, bringing to awareness your senses,
thus, allowing you to notice your surroundings
while giving you a deep sense of peace. If possible, find a
nearby tree that you can connect with and visit often as a friend.

What is your favorite form of exercise? Take a moment to
move in a way that releases pent up feelings. Now how do
you feel? Write or create a drawing about this experience.
Journal about how it makes you feel before, during,
and after some form of movement, like taking a walk,
dancing, swimming, doing yoga, etc.

How does exercise and being outdoors affect your digestion?

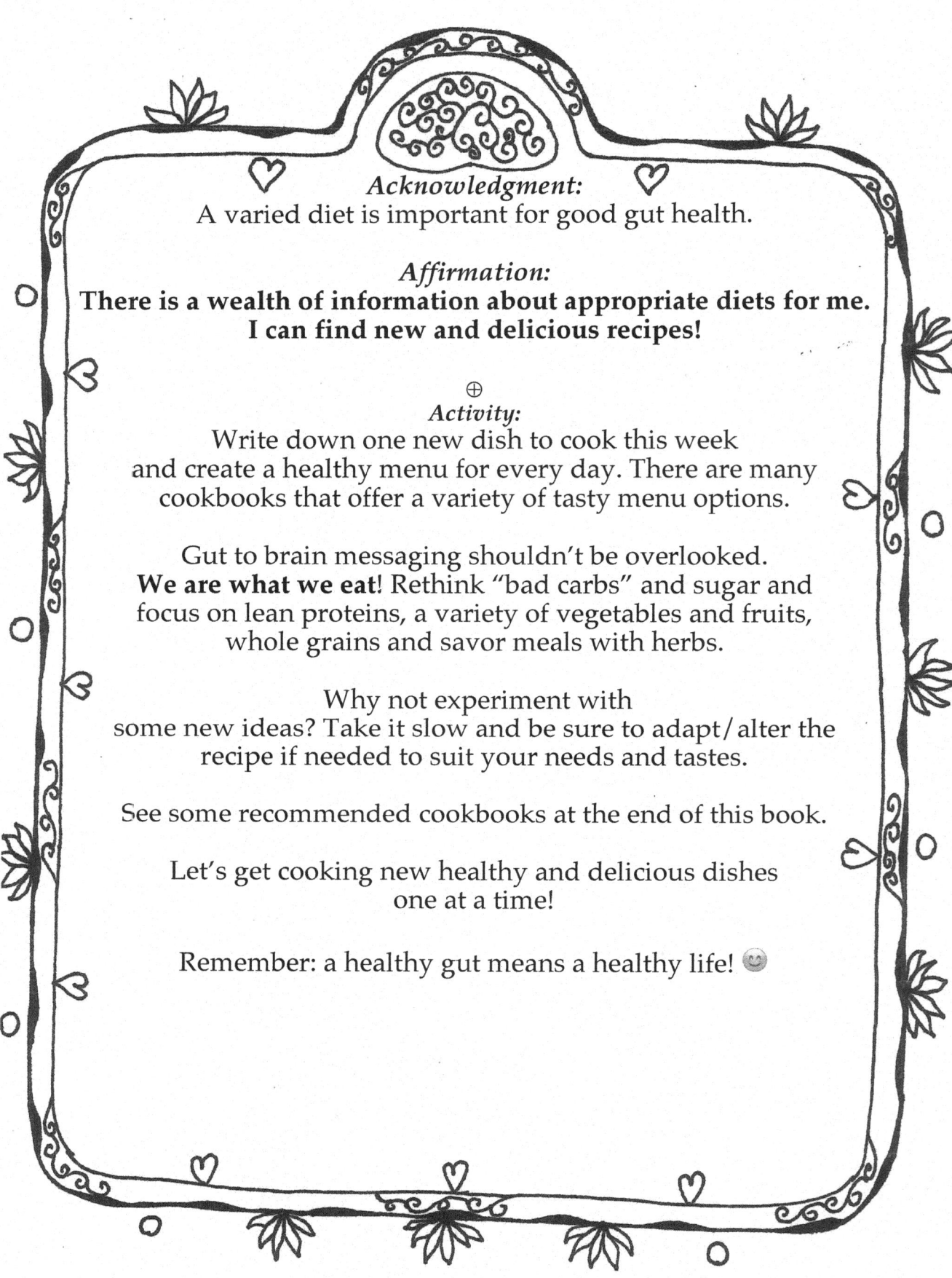

Acknowledgment:
A varied diet is important for good gut health.

Affirmation:
**There is a wealth of information about appropriate diets for me.
I can find new and delicious recipes!**

⊕

Activity:
Write down one new dish to cook this week
and create a healthy menu for every day. There are many
cookbooks that offer a variety of tasty menu options.

Gut to brain messaging shouldn't be overlooked.
We are what we eat! Rethink "bad carbs" and sugar and
focus on lean proteins, a variety of vegetables and fruits,
whole grains and savor meals with herbs.

Why not experiment with
some new ideas? Take it slow and be sure to adapt/alter the
recipe if needed to suit your needs and tastes.

See some recommended cookbooks at the end of this book.

Let's get cooking new healthy and delicious dishes
one at a time!

Remember: a healthy gut means a healthy life! 😊

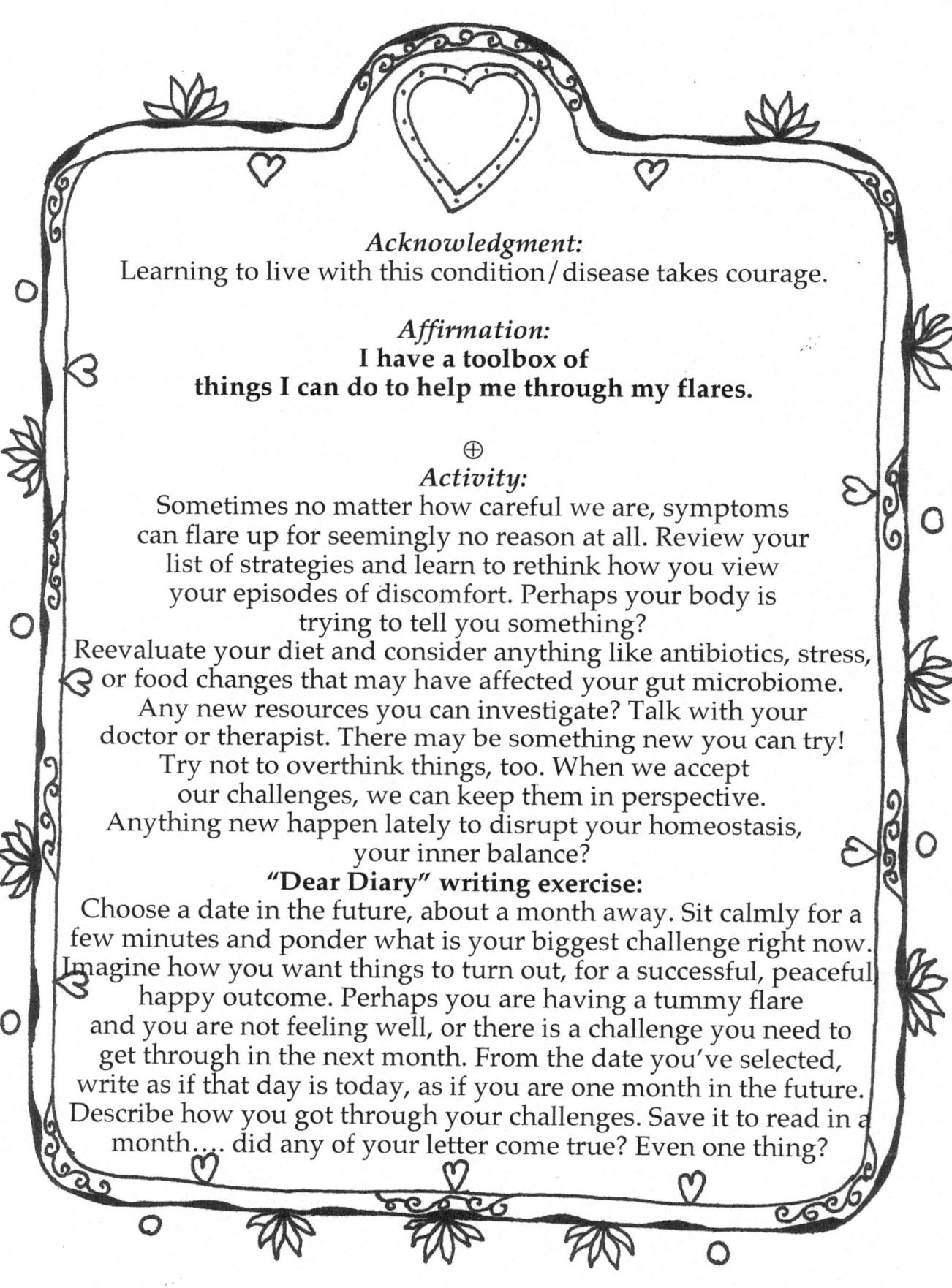

Acknowledgment:
Learning to live with this condition/disease takes courage.

Affirmation:
**I have a toolbox of
things I can do to help me through my flares.**

⊕
Activity:
Sometimes no matter how careful we are, symptoms
can flare up for seemingly no reason at all. Review your
list of strategies and learn to rethink how you view
your episodes of discomfort. Perhaps your body is
trying to tell you something?
Reevaluate your diet and consider anything like antibiotics, stress,
or food changes that may have affected your gut microbiome.
Any new resources you can investigate? Talk with your
doctor or therapist. There may be something new you can try!
Try not to overthink things, too. When we accept
our challenges, we can keep them in perspective.
Anything new happen lately to disrupt your homeostasis,
your inner balance?

"Dear Diary" writing exercise:
Choose a date in the future, about a month away. Sit calmly for a
few minutes and ponder what is your biggest challenge right now.
Imagine how you want things to turn out, for a successful, peaceful
happy outcome. Perhaps you are having a tummy flare
and you are not feeling well, or there is a challenge you need to
get through in the next month. From the date you've selected,
write as if that day is today, as if you are one month in the future.
Describe how you got through your challenges. Save it to read in a
month…. did any of your letter come true? Even one thing?

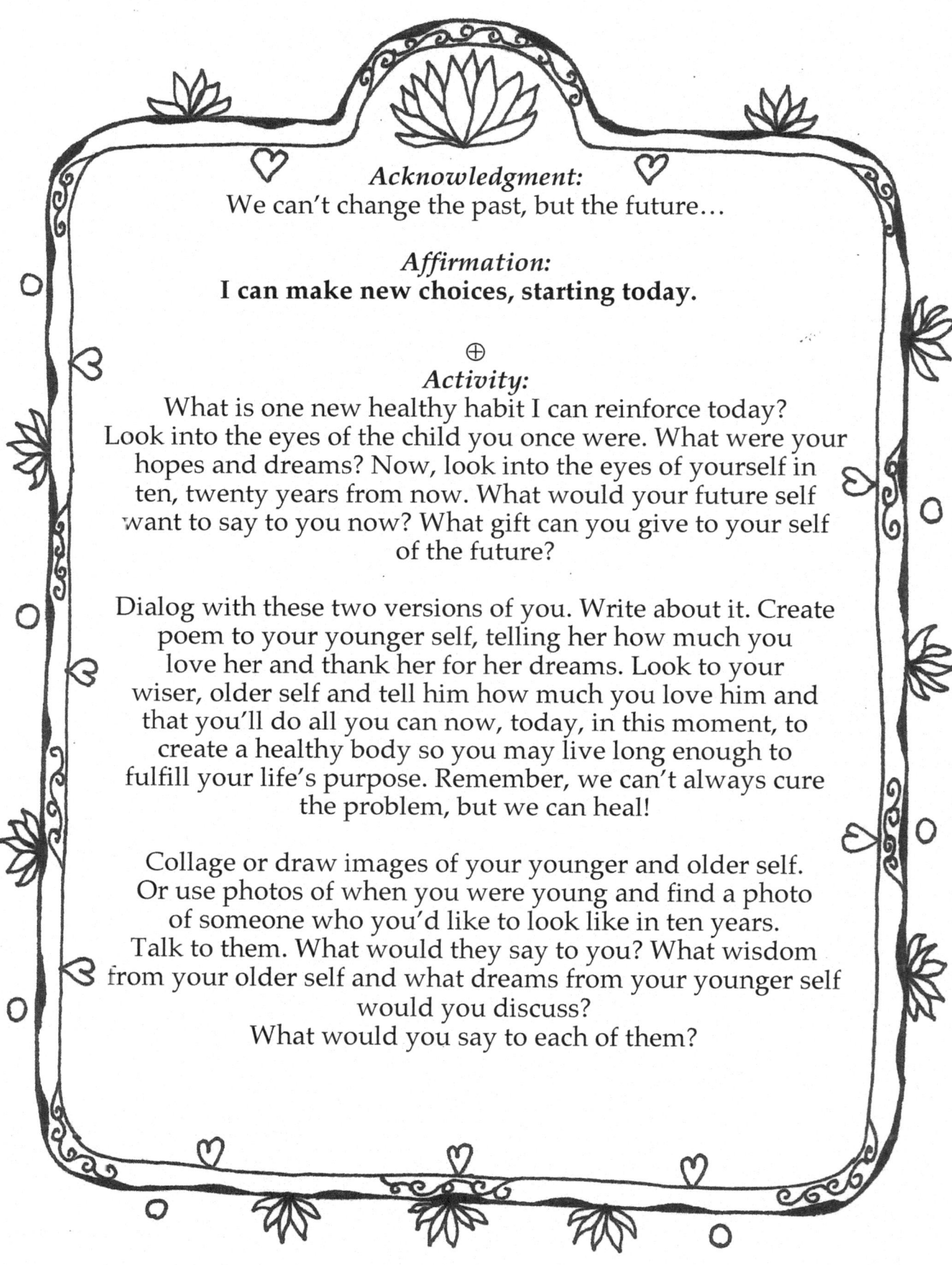

Acknowledgment:
We can't change the past, but the future...

Affirmation:
I can make new choices, starting today.

⊕

Activity:
What is one new healthy habit I can reinforce today?
Look into the eyes of the child you once were. What were your
hopes and dreams? Now, look into the eyes of yourself in
ten, twenty years from now. What would your future self
want to say to you now? What gift can you give to your self
of the future?

Dialog with these two versions of you. Write about it. Create
poem to your younger self, telling her how much you
love her and thank her for her dreams. Look to your
wiser, older self and tell him how much you love him and
that you'll do all you can now, today, in this moment, to
create a healthy body so you may live long enough to
fulfill your life's purpose. Remember, we can't always cure
the problem, but we can heal!

Collage or draw images of your younger and older self.
Or use photos of when you were young and find a photo
of someone who you'd like to look like in ten years.
Talk to them. What would they say to you? What wisdom
from your older self and what dreams from your younger self
would you discuss?
What would you say to each of them?

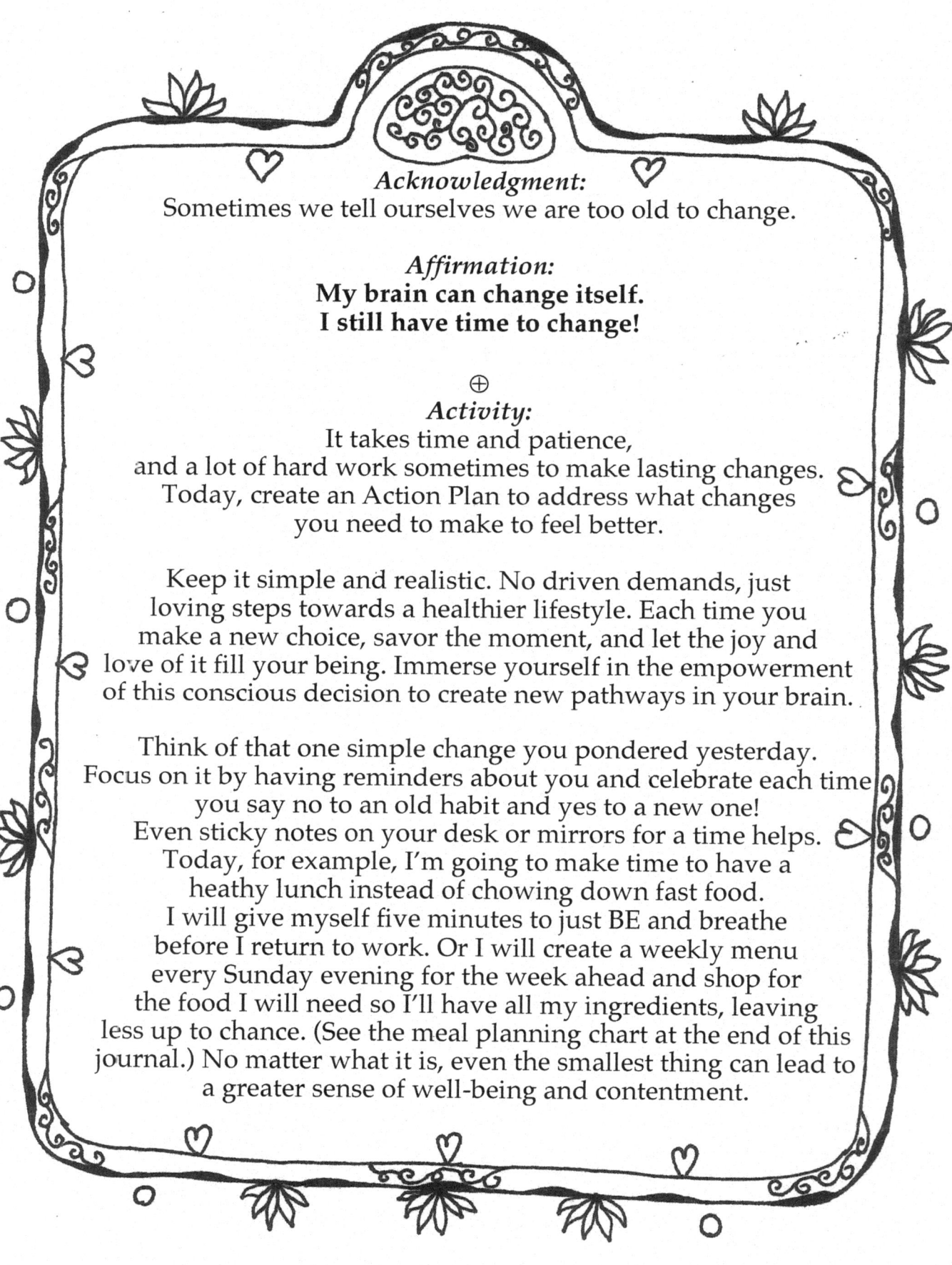

Acknowledgment:
Sometimes we tell ourselves we are too old to change.

Affirmation:
My brain can change itself.
I still have time to change!

⊕

Activity:
It takes time and patience,
and a lot of hard work sometimes to make lasting changes.
Today, create an Action Plan to address what changes
you need to make to feel better.

Keep it simple and realistic. No driven demands, just
loving steps towards a healthier lifestyle. Each time you
make a new choice, savor the moment, and let the joy and
love of it fill your being. Immerse yourself in the empowerment
of this conscious decision to create new pathways in your brain.

Think of that one simple change you pondered yesterday.
Focus on it by having reminders about you and celebrate each time
you say no to an old habit and yes to a new one!
Even sticky notes on your desk or mirrors for a time helps.
Today, for example, I'm going to make time to have a
heathy lunch instead of chowing down fast food.
I will give myself five minutes to just BE and breathe
before I return to work. Or I will create a weekly menu
every Sunday evening for the week ahead and shop for
the food I will need so I'll have all my ingredients, leaving
less up to chance. (See the meal planning chart at the end of this
journal.) No matter what it is, even the smallest thing can lead to
a greater sense of well-being and contentment.

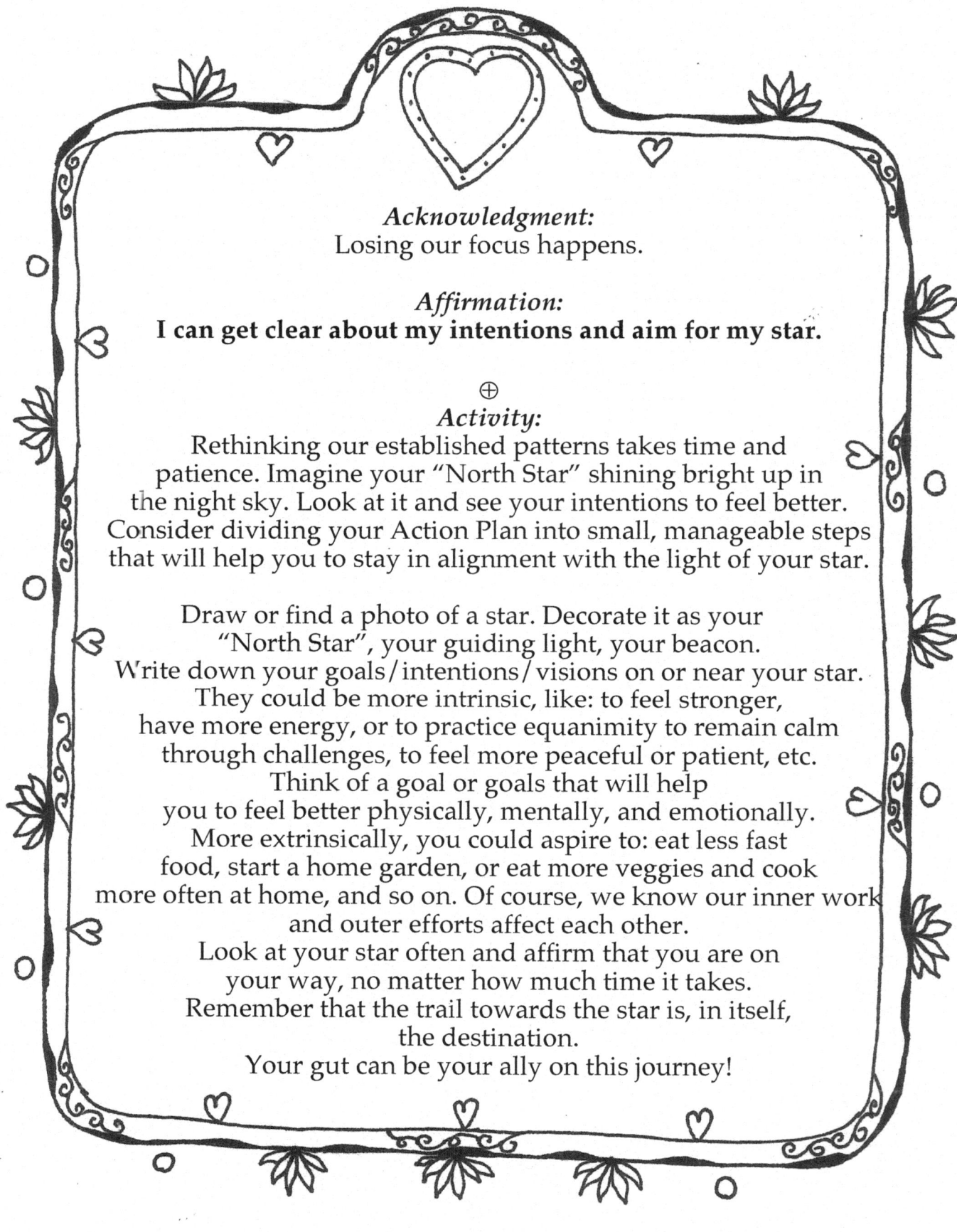

Acknowledgment:
Losing our focus happens.

Affirmation:
I can get clear about my intentions and aim for my star.

⊕

Activity:
Rethinking our established patterns takes time and
patience. Imagine your "North Star" shining bright up in
the night sky. Look at it and see your intentions to feel better.
Consider dividing your Action Plan into small, manageable steps
that will help you to stay in alignment with the light of your star.

Draw or find a photo of a star. Decorate it as your
"North Star", your guiding light, your beacon.
Write down your goals/intentions/visions on or near your star.
They could be more intrinsic, like: to feel stronger,
have more energy, or to practice equanimity to remain calm
through challenges, to feel more peaceful or patient, etc.
Think of a goal or goals that will help
you to feel better physically, mentally, and emotionally.
More extrinsically, you could aspire to: eat less fast
food, start a home garden, or eat more veggies and cook
more often at home, and so on. Of course, we know our inner work
and outer efforts affect each other.
Look at your star often and affirm that you are on
your way, no matter how much time it takes.
Remember that the trail towards the star is, in itself,
the destination.
Your gut can be your ally on this journey!

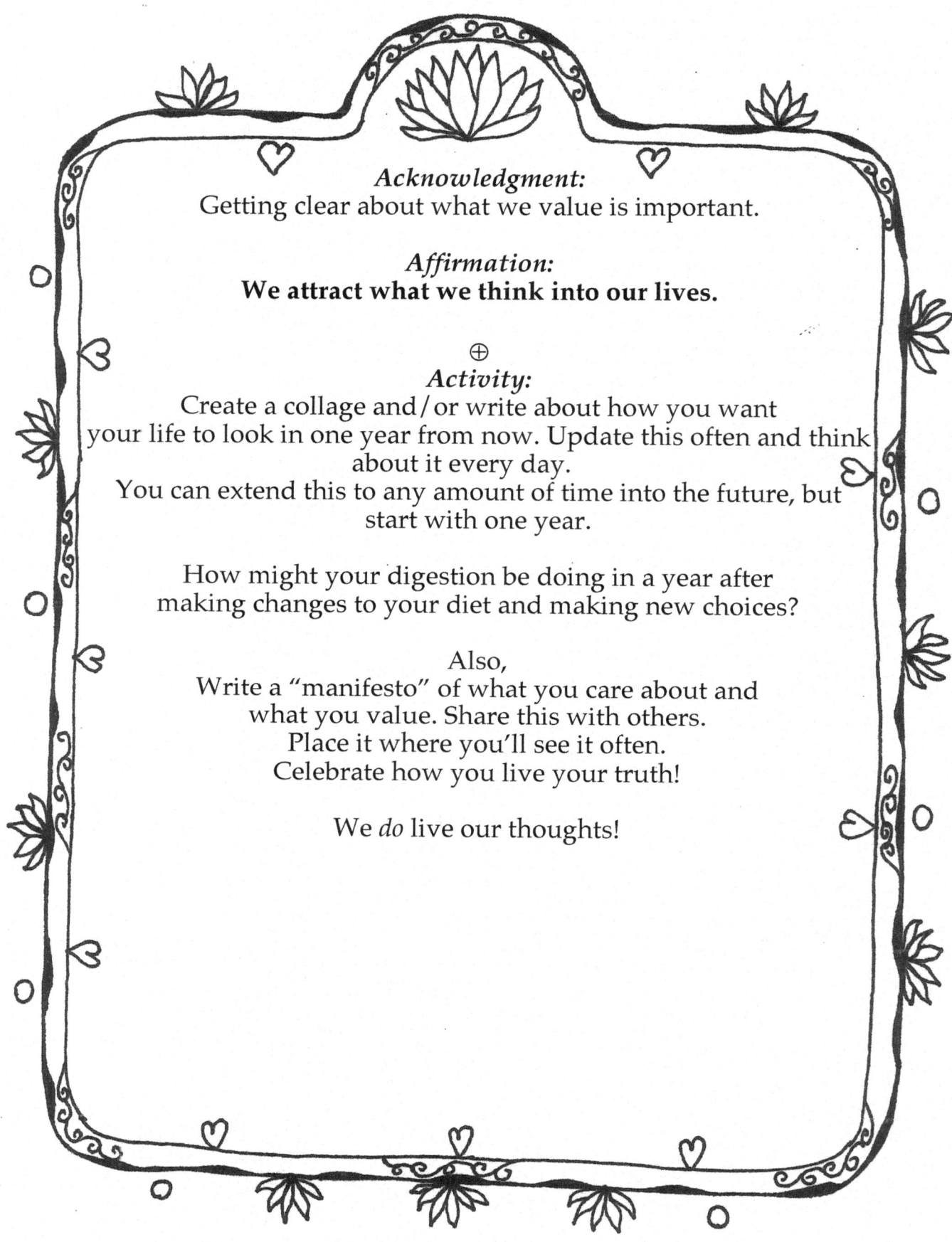

Acknowledgment:
Getting clear about what we value is important.

Affirmation:
We attract what we think into our lives.

⊕

Activity:
Create a collage and/or write about how you want
your life to look in one year from now. Update this often and think
about it every day.
You can extend this to any amount of time into the future, but
start with one year.

How might your digestion be doing in a year after
making changes to your diet and making new choices?

Also,
Write a "manifesto" of what you care about and
what you value. Share this with others.
Place it where you'll see it often.
Celebrate how you live your truth!

We *do* live our thoughts!

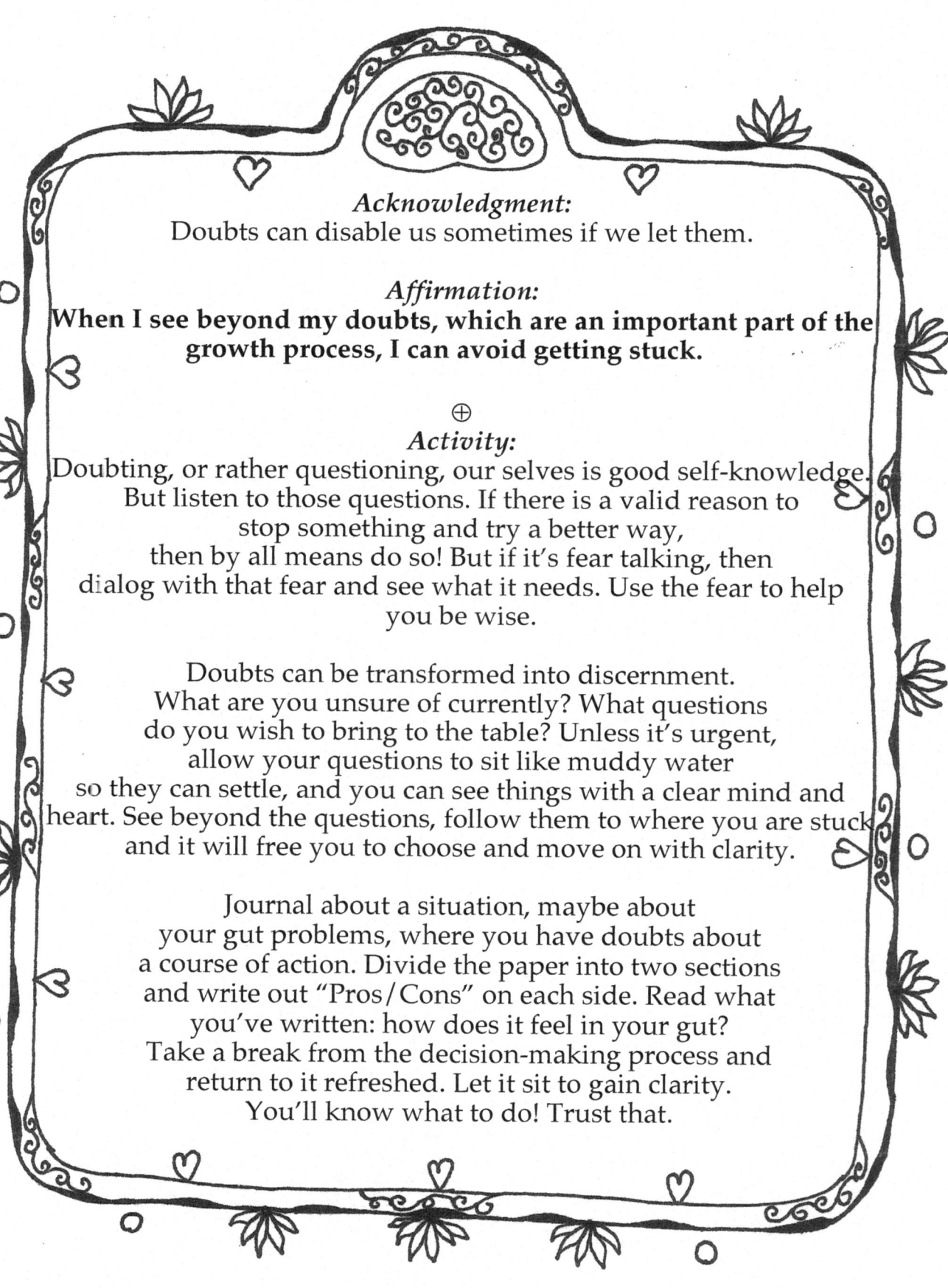

Acknowledgment:
Doubts can disable us sometimes if we let them.

Affirmation:
When I see beyond my doubts, which are an important part of the growth process, I can avoid getting stuck.

⊕

Activity:
Doubting, or rather questioning, our selves is good self-knowledge.
But listen to those questions. If there is a valid reason to
stop something and try a better way,
then by all means do so! But if it's fear talking, then
dialog with that fear and see what it needs. Use the fear to help
you be wise.

Doubts can be transformed into discernment.
What are you unsure of currently? What questions
do you wish to bring to the table? Unless it's urgent,
allow your questions to sit like muddy water
so they can settle, and you can see things with a clear mind and
heart. See beyond the questions, follow them to where you are stuck
and it will free you to choose and move on with clarity.

Journal about a situation, maybe about
your gut problems, where you have doubts about
a course of action. Divide the paper into two sections
and write out "Pros/Cons" on each side. Read what
you've written: how does it feel in your gut?
Take a break from the decision-making process and
return to it refreshed. Let it sit to gain clarity.
You'll know what to do! Trust that.

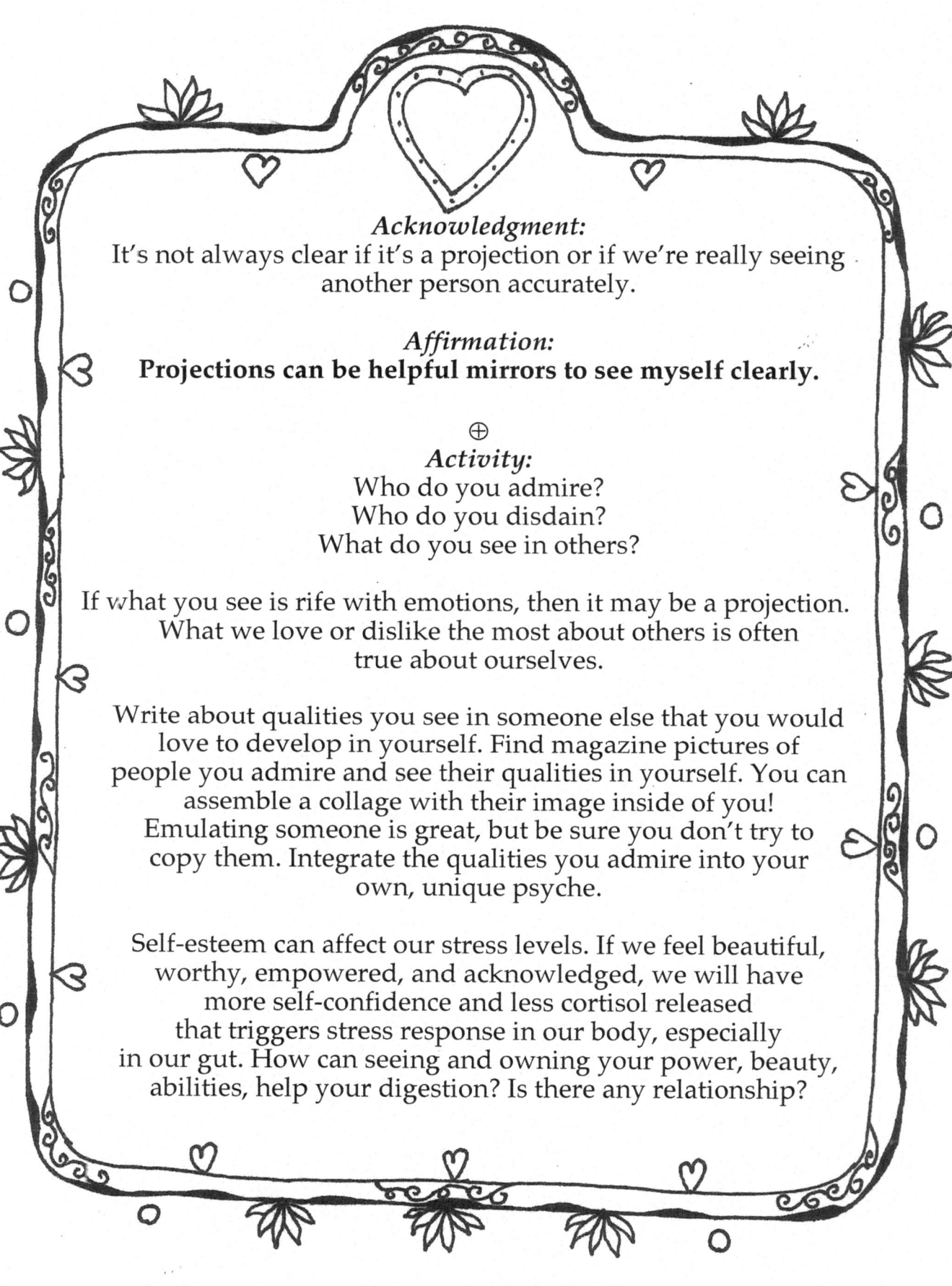

Acknowledgment:
It's not always clear if it's a projection or if we're really seeing
another person accurately.

Affirmation:
Projections can be helpful mirrors to see myself clearly.

⊕
Activity:
Who do you admire?
Who do you disdain?
What do you see in others?

If what you see is rife with emotions, then it may be a projection.
What we love or dislike the most about others is often
true about ourselves.

Write about qualities you see in someone else that you would
love to develop in yourself. Find magazine pictures of
people you admire and see their qualities in yourself. You can
assemble a collage with their image inside of you!
Emulating someone is great, but be sure you don't try to
copy them. Integrate the qualities you admire into your
own, unique psyche.

Self-esteem can affect our stress levels. If we feel beautiful,
worthy, empowered, and acknowledged, we will have
more self-confidence and less cortisol released
that triggers stress response in our body, especially
in our gut. How can seeing and owning your power, beauty,
abilities, help your digestion? Is there any relationship?

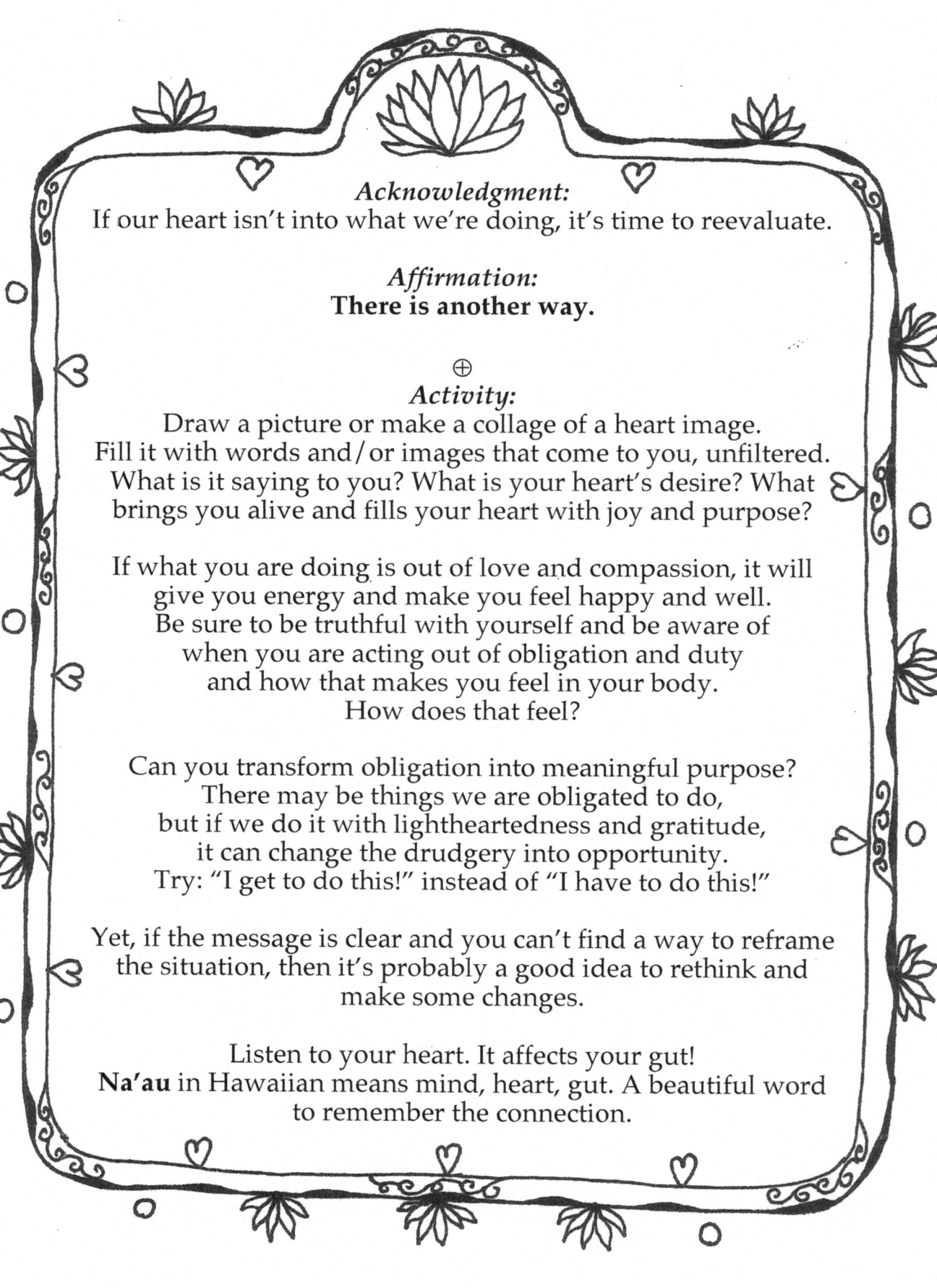

Acknowledgment:
If our heart isn't into what we're doing, it's time to reevaluate.

Affirmation:
There is another way.

⊕

Activity:
Draw a picture or make a collage of a heart image.
Fill it with words and/or images that come to you, unfiltered.
What is it saying to you? What is your heart's desire? What
brings you alive and fills your heart with joy and purpose?

If what you are doing is out of love and compassion, it will
give you energy and make you feel happy and well.
Be sure to be truthful with yourself and be aware of
when you are acting out of obligation and duty
and how that makes you feel in your body.
How does that feel?

Can you transform obligation into meaningful purpose?
There may be things we are obligated to do,
but if we do it with lightheartedness and gratitude,
it can change the drudgery into opportunity.
Try: "I get to do this!" instead of "I have to do this!"

Yet, if the message is clear and you can't find a way to reframe
the situation, then it's probably a good idea to rethink and
make some changes.

Listen to your heart. It affects your gut!
Na'au in Hawaiian means mind, heart, gut. A beautiful word
to remember the connection.

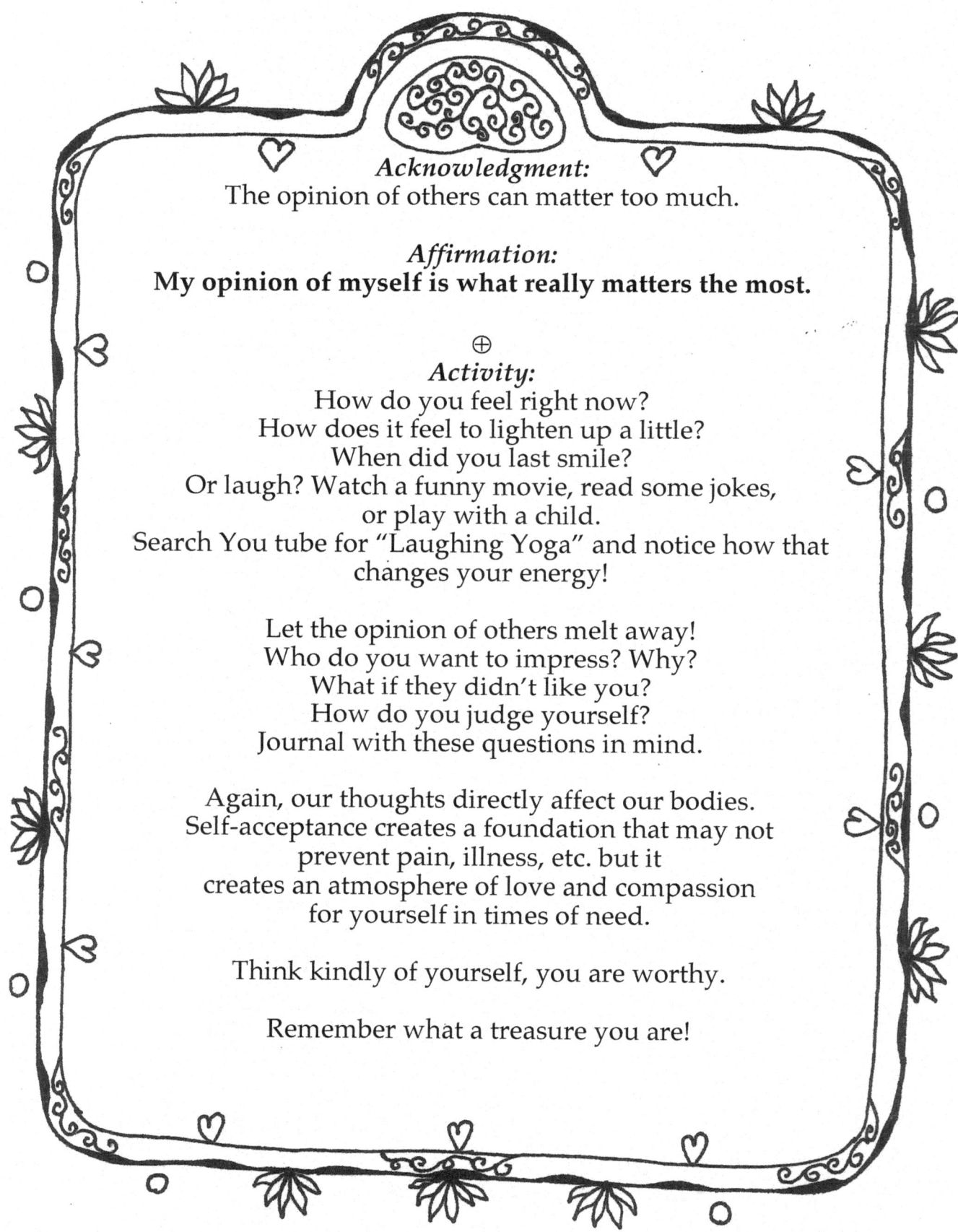

Acknowledgment:
The opinion of others can matter too much.

Affirmation:
My opinion of myself is what really matters the most.

⊕

Activity:
How do you feel right now?
How does it feel to lighten up a little?
When did you last smile?
Or laugh? Watch a funny movie, read some jokes,
or play with a child.
Search You tube for "Laughing Yoga" and notice how that
changes your energy!

Let the opinion of others melt away!
Who do you want to impress? Why?
What if they didn't like you?
How do you judge yourself?
Journal with these questions in mind.

Again, our thoughts directly affect our bodies.
Self-acceptance creates a foundation that may not
prevent pain, illness, etc. but it
creates an atmosphere of love and compassion
for yourself in times of need.

Think kindly of yourself, you are worthy.

Remember what a treasure you are!

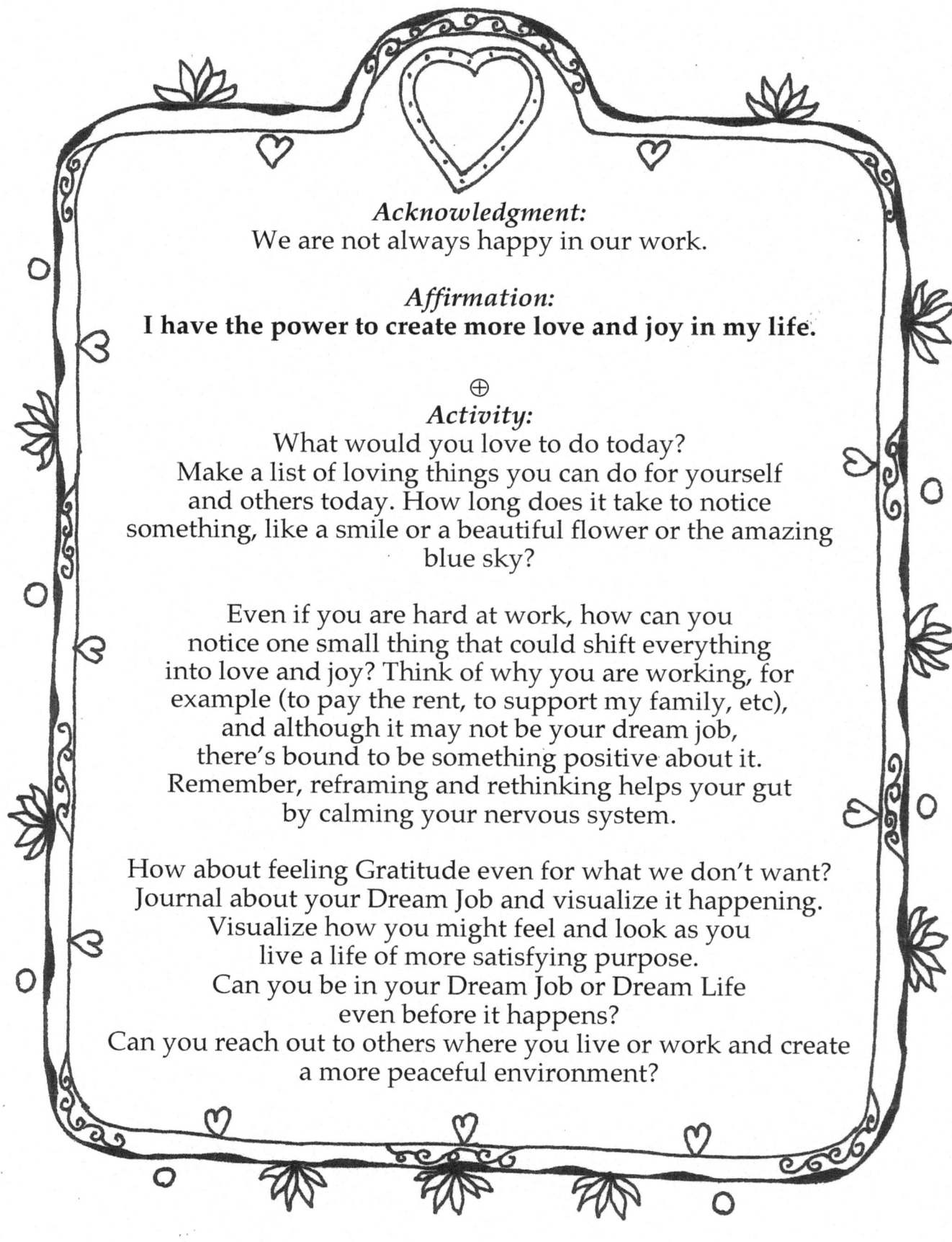

Acknowledgment:
We are not always happy in our work.

Affirmation:
I have the power to create more love and joy in my life.

⊕
Activity:
What would you love to do today?
Make a list of loving things you can do for yourself
and others today. How long does it take to notice
something, like a smile or a beautiful flower or the amazing
blue sky?

Even if you are hard at work, how can you
notice one small thing that could shift everything
into love and joy? Think of why you are working, for
example (to pay the rent, to support my family, etc),
and although it may not be your dream job,
there's bound to be something positive about it.
Remember, reframing and rethinking helps your gut
by calming your nervous system.

How about feeling Gratitude even for what we don't want?
Journal about your Dream Job and visualize it happening.
Visualize how you might feel and look as you
live a life of more satisfying purpose.
Can you be in your Dream Job or Dream Life
even before it happens?
Can you reach out to others where you live or work and create
a more peaceful environment?

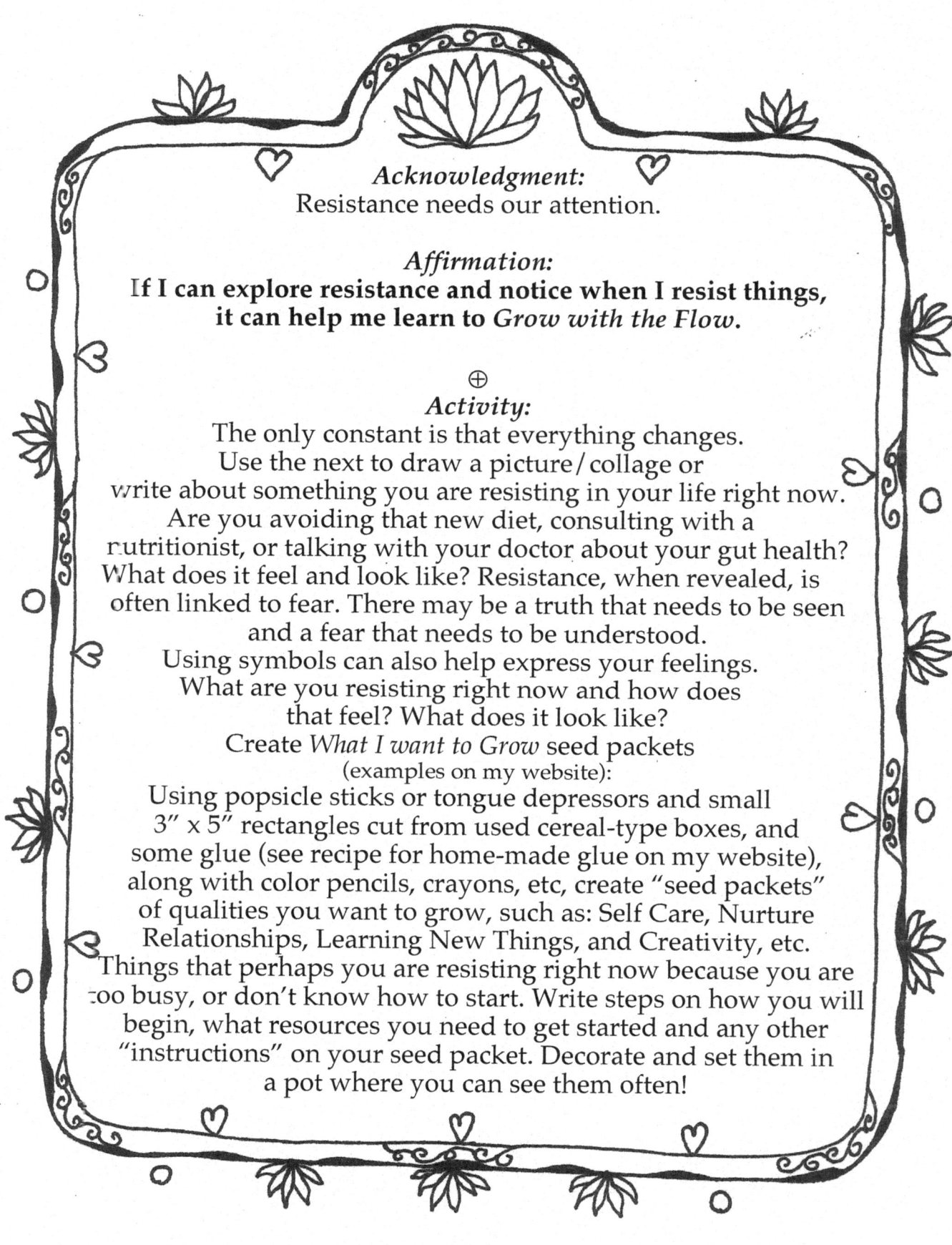

Acknowledgment:
Resistance needs our attention.

Affirmation:
**If I can explore resistance and notice when I resist things,
it can help me learn to *Grow with the Flow*.**

⊕

Activity:
The only constant is that everything changes.
Use the next to draw a picture/collage or
write about something you are resisting in your life right now.
Are you avoiding that new diet, consulting with a
nutritionist, or talking with your doctor about your gut health?
What does it feel and look like? Resistance, when revealed, is
often linked to fear. There may be a truth that needs to be seen
and a fear that needs to be understood.
Using symbols can also help express your feelings.
What are you resisting right now and how does
that feel? What does it look like?
Create *What I want to Grow* seed packets
(examples on my website):
Using popsicle sticks or tongue depressors and small
3″ x 5″ rectangles cut from used cereal-type boxes, and
some glue (see recipe for home-made glue on my website),
along with color pencils, crayons, etc, create "seed packets"
of qualities you want to grow, such as: Self Care, Nurture
Relationships, Learning New Things, and Creativity, etc.
Things that perhaps you are resisting right now because you are
too busy, or don't know how to start. Write steps on how you will
begin, what resources you need to get started and any other
"instructions" on your seed packet. Decorate and set them in
a pot where you can see them often!

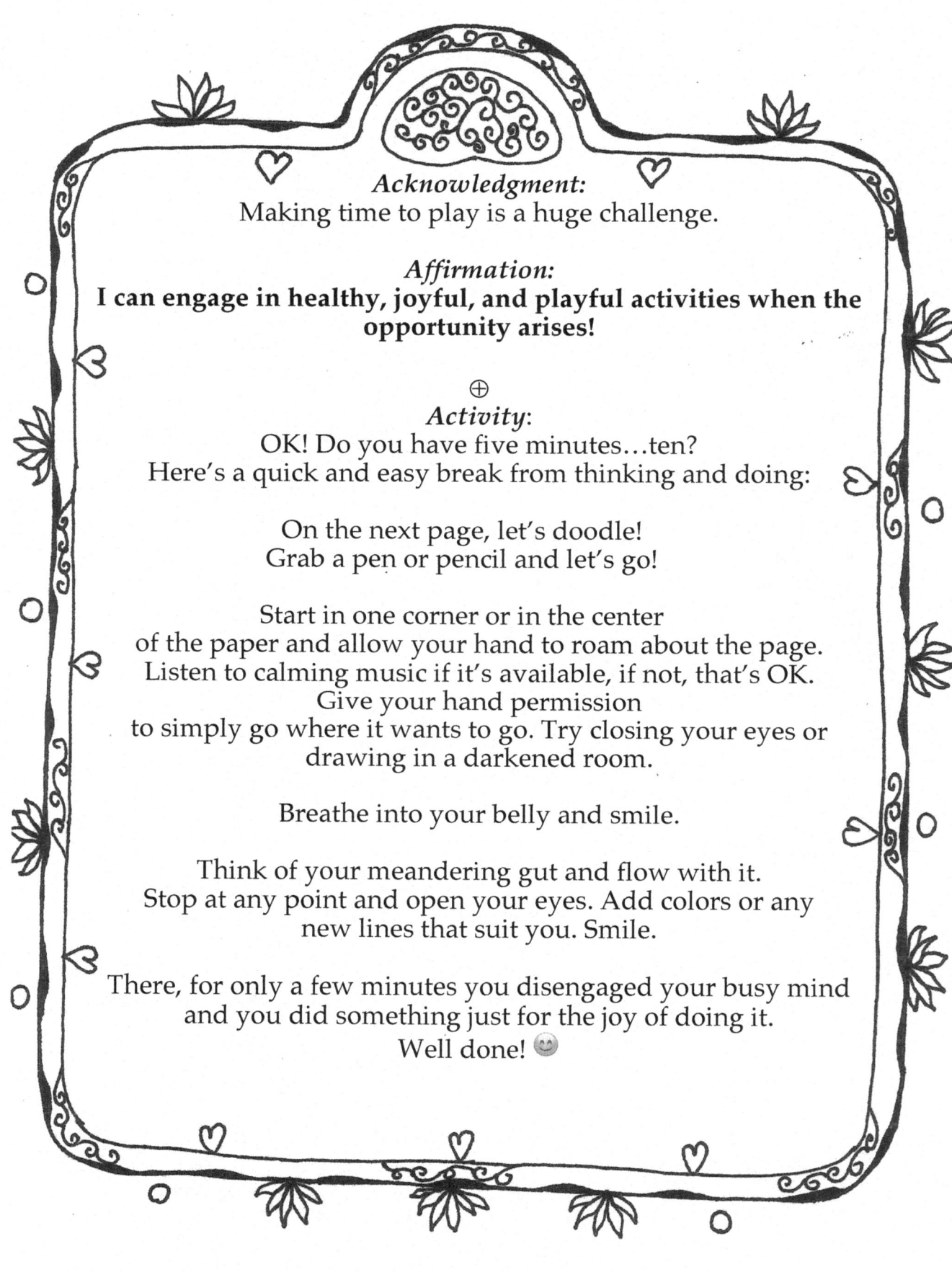

Acknowledgment:
Making time to play is a huge challenge.

Affirmation:
I can engage in healthy, joyful, and playful activities when the opportunity arises!

⊕

Activity:
OK! Do you have five minutes...ten?
Here's a quick and easy break from thinking and doing:

On the next page, let's doodle!
Grab a pen or pencil and let's go!

Start in one corner or in the center
of the paper and allow your hand to roam about the page.
Listen to calming music if it's available, if not, that's OK.
Give your hand permission
to simply go where it wants to go. Try closing your eyes or
drawing in a darkened room.

Breathe into your belly and smile.

Think of your meandering gut and flow with it.
Stop at any point and open your eyes. Add colors or any
new lines that suit you. Smile.

There, for only a few minutes you disengaged your busy mind
and you did something just for the joy of doing it.
Well done! 😊

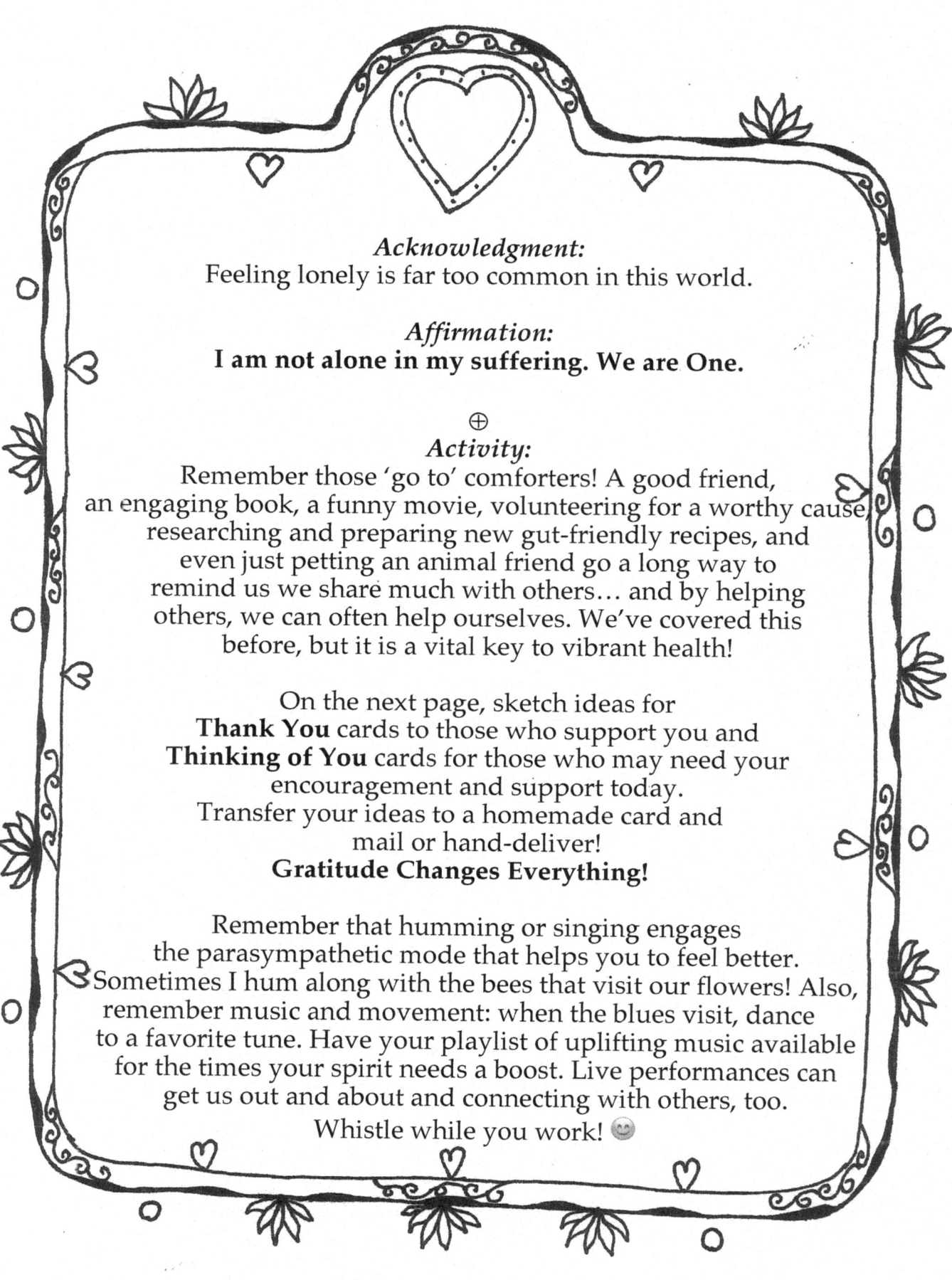

Acknowledgment:
Feeling lonely is far too common in this world.

Affirmation:
I am not alone in my suffering. We are One.

⊕
Activity:
Remember those 'go to' comforters! A good friend,
an engaging book, a funny movie, volunteering for a worthy cause,
researching and preparing new gut-friendly recipes, and
even just petting an animal friend go a long way to
remind us we share much with others… and by helping
others, we can often help ourselves. We've covered this
before, but it is a vital key to vibrant health!

On the next page, sketch ideas for
Thank You cards to those who support you and
Thinking of You cards for those who may need your
encouragement and support today.
Transfer your ideas to a homemade card and
mail or hand-deliver!
Gratitude Changes Everything!

Remember that humming or singing engages
the parasympathetic mode that helps you to feel better.
Sometimes I hum along with the bees that visit our flowers! Also,
remember music and movement: when the blues visit, dance
to a favorite tune. Have your playlist of uplifting music available
for the times your spirit needs a boost. Live performances can
get us out and about and connecting with others, too.
Whistle while you work! 😊

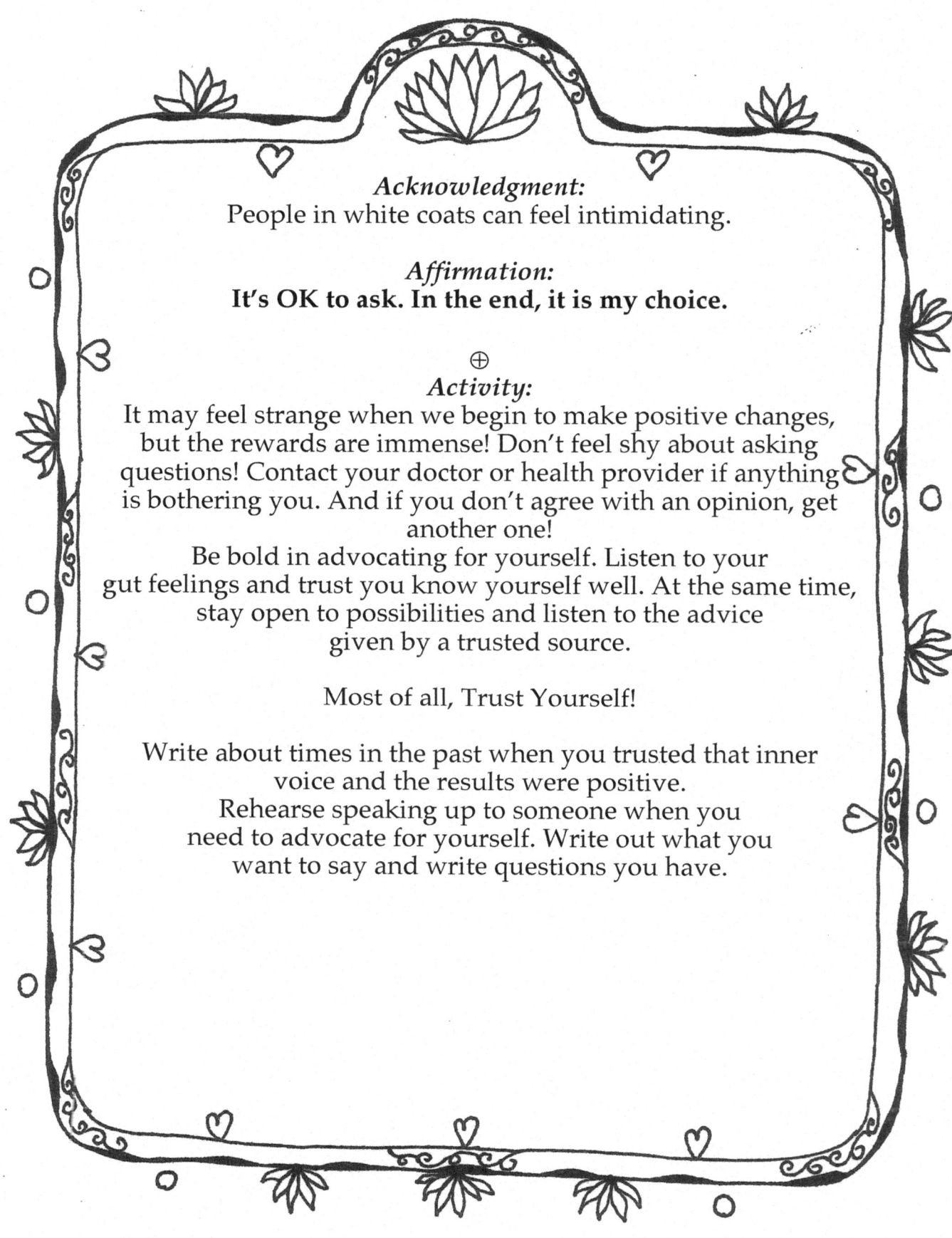

Acknowledgment:
People in white coats can feel intimidating.

Affirmation:
It's OK to ask. In the end, it is my choice.

⊕

Activity:
It may feel strange when we begin to make positive changes,
but the rewards are immense! Don't feel shy about asking
questions! Contact your doctor or health provider if anything
is bothering you. And if you don't agree with an opinion, get
another one!
Be bold in advocating for yourself. Listen to your
gut feelings and trust you know yourself well. At the same time,
stay open to possibilities and listen to the advice
given by a trusted source.

Most of all, Trust Yourself!

Write about times in the past when you trusted that inner
voice and the results were positive.
Rehearse speaking up to someone when you
need to advocate for yourself. Write out what you
want to say and write questions you have.

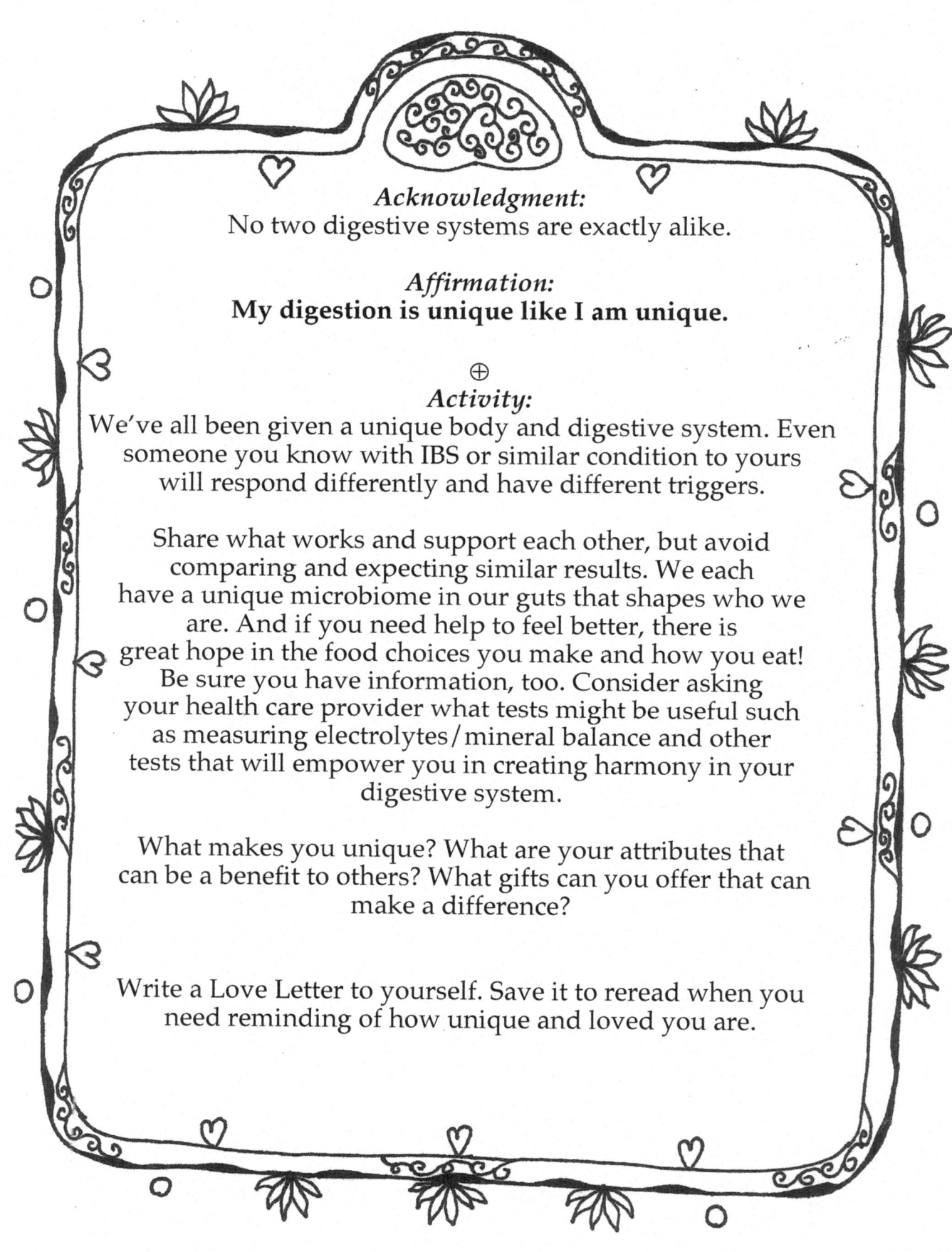

Acknowledgment:
No two digestive systems are exactly alike.

Affirmation:
My digestion is unique like I am unique.

⊕

Activity:
We've all been given a unique body and digestive system. Even someone you know with IBS or similar condition to yours will respond differently and have different triggers.

Share what works and support each other, but avoid comparing and expecting similar results. We each have a unique microbiome in our guts that shapes who we are. And if you need help to feel better, there is great hope in the food choices you make and how you eat! Be sure you have information, too. Consider asking your health care provider what tests might be useful such as measuring electrolytes / mineral balance and other tests that will empower you in creating harmony in your digestive system.

What makes you unique? What are your attributes that can be a benefit to others? What gifts can you offer that can make a difference?

Write a Love Letter to yourself. Save it to reread when you need reminding of how unique and loved you are.

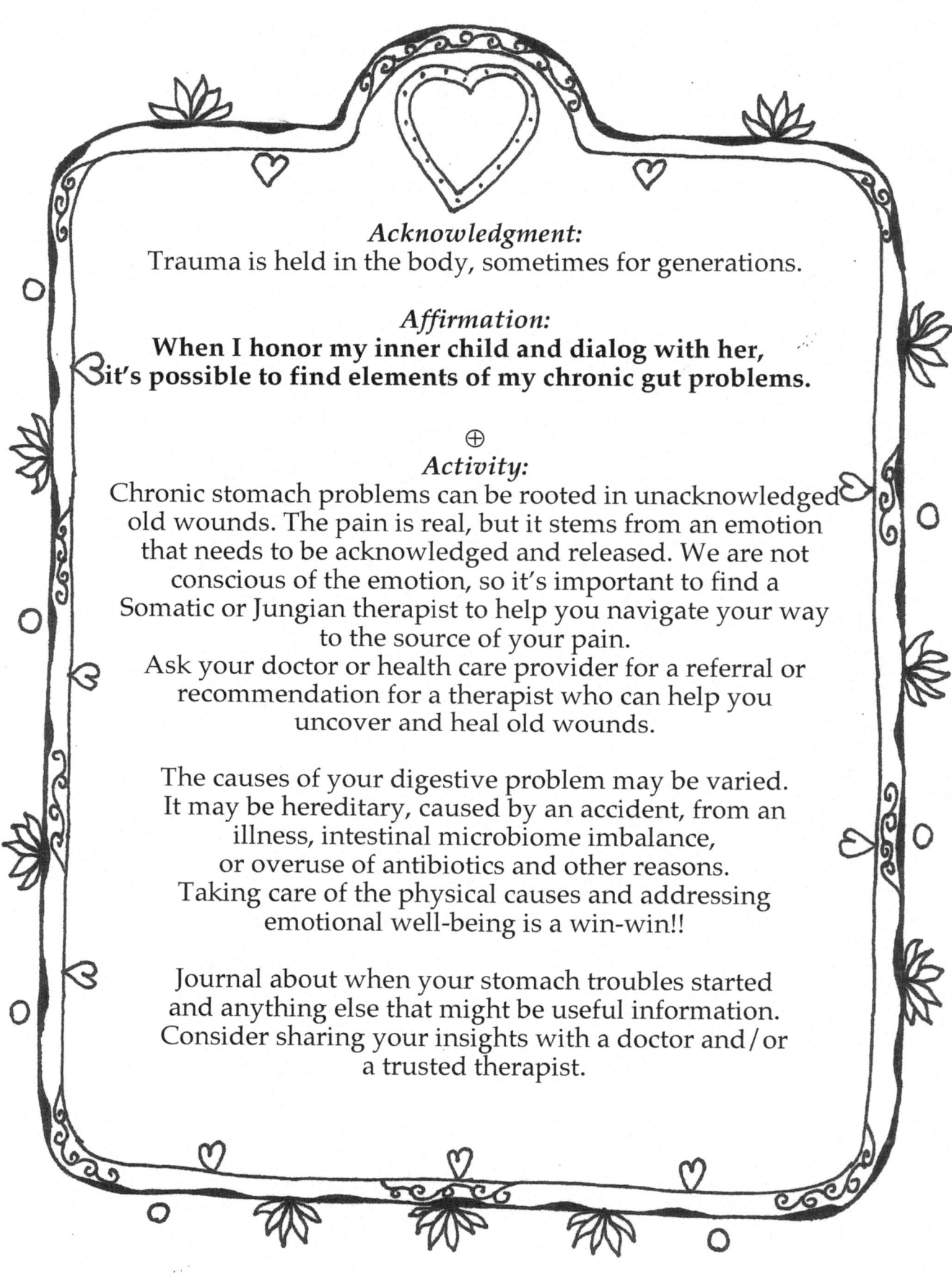

Acknowledgment:
Trauma is held in the body, sometimes for generations.

Affirmation:
**When I honor my inner child and dialog with her,
it's possible to find elements of my chronic gut problems.**

⊕

Activity:
Chronic stomach problems can be rooted in unacknowledged
old wounds. The pain is real, but it stems from an emotion
that needs to be acknowledged and released. We are not
conscious of the emotion, so it's important to find a
Somatic or Jungian therapist to help you navigate your way
to the source of your pain.
Ask your doctor or health care provider for a referral or
recommendation for a therapist who can help you
uncover and heal old wounds.

The causes of your digestive problem may be varied.
It may be hereditary, caused by an accident, from an
illness, intestinal microbiome imbalance,
or overuse of antibiotics and other reasons.
Taking care of the physical causes and addressing
emotional well-being is a win-win!!

Journal about when your stomach troubles started
and anything else that might be useful information.
Consider sharing your insights with a doctor and/or
a trusted therapist.

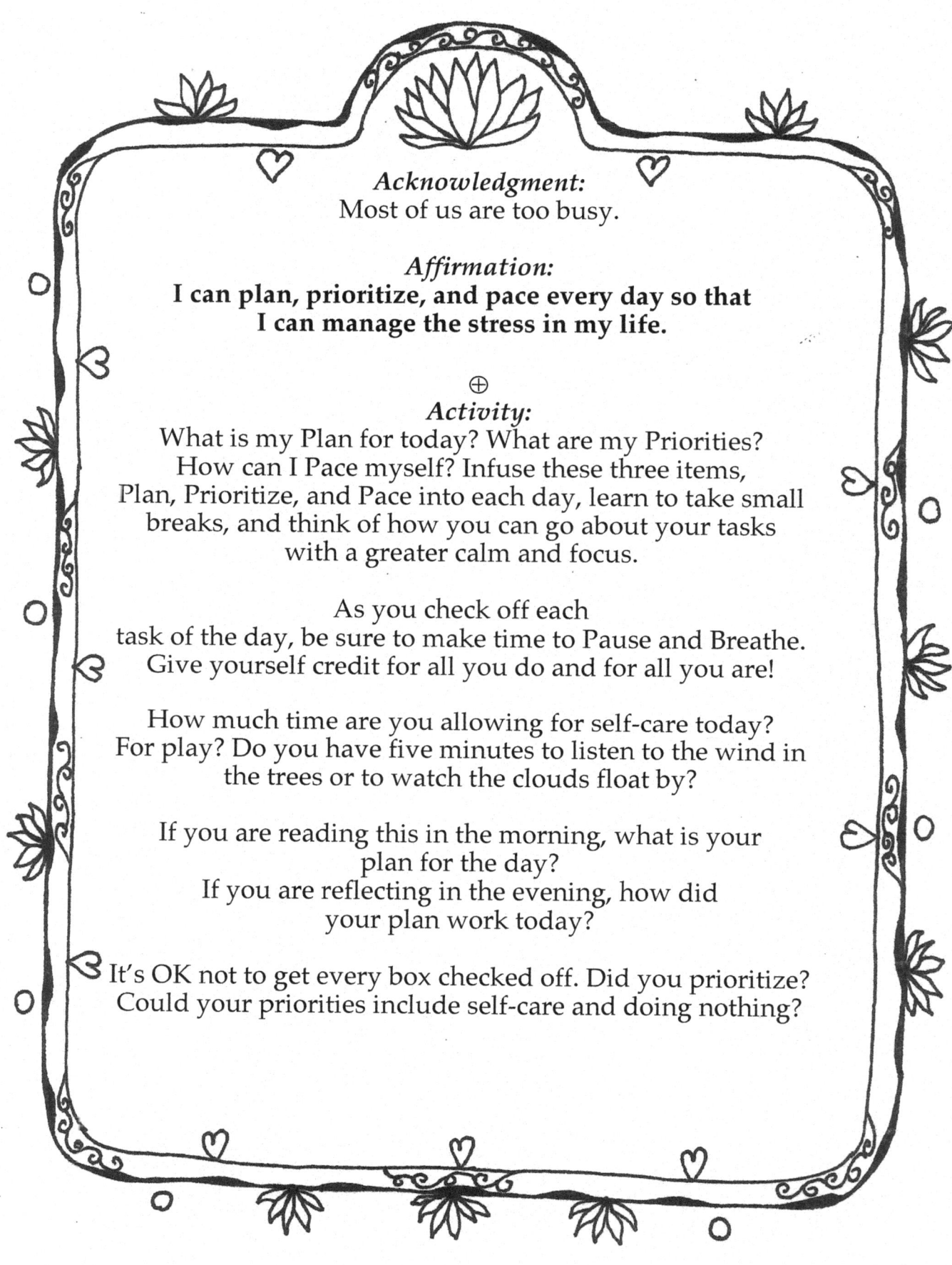

Acknowledgment:
Most of us are too busy.

Affirmation:
**I can plan, prioritize, and pace every day so that
I can manage the stress in my life.**

⊕

Activity:
What is my Plan for today? What are my Priorities?
How can I Pace myself? Infuse these three items,
Plan, Prioritize, and Pace into each day, learn to take small
breaks, and think of how you can go about your tasks
with a greater calm and focus.

As you check off each
task of the day, be sure to make time to Pause and Breathe.
Give yourself credit for all you do and for all you are!

How much time are you allowing for self-care today?
For play? Do you have five minutes to listen to the wind in
the trees or to watch the clouds float by?

If you are reading this in the morning, what is your
plan for the day?
If you are reflecting in the evening, how did
your plan work today?

It's OK not to get every box checked off. Did you prioritize?
Could your priorities include self-care and doing nothing?

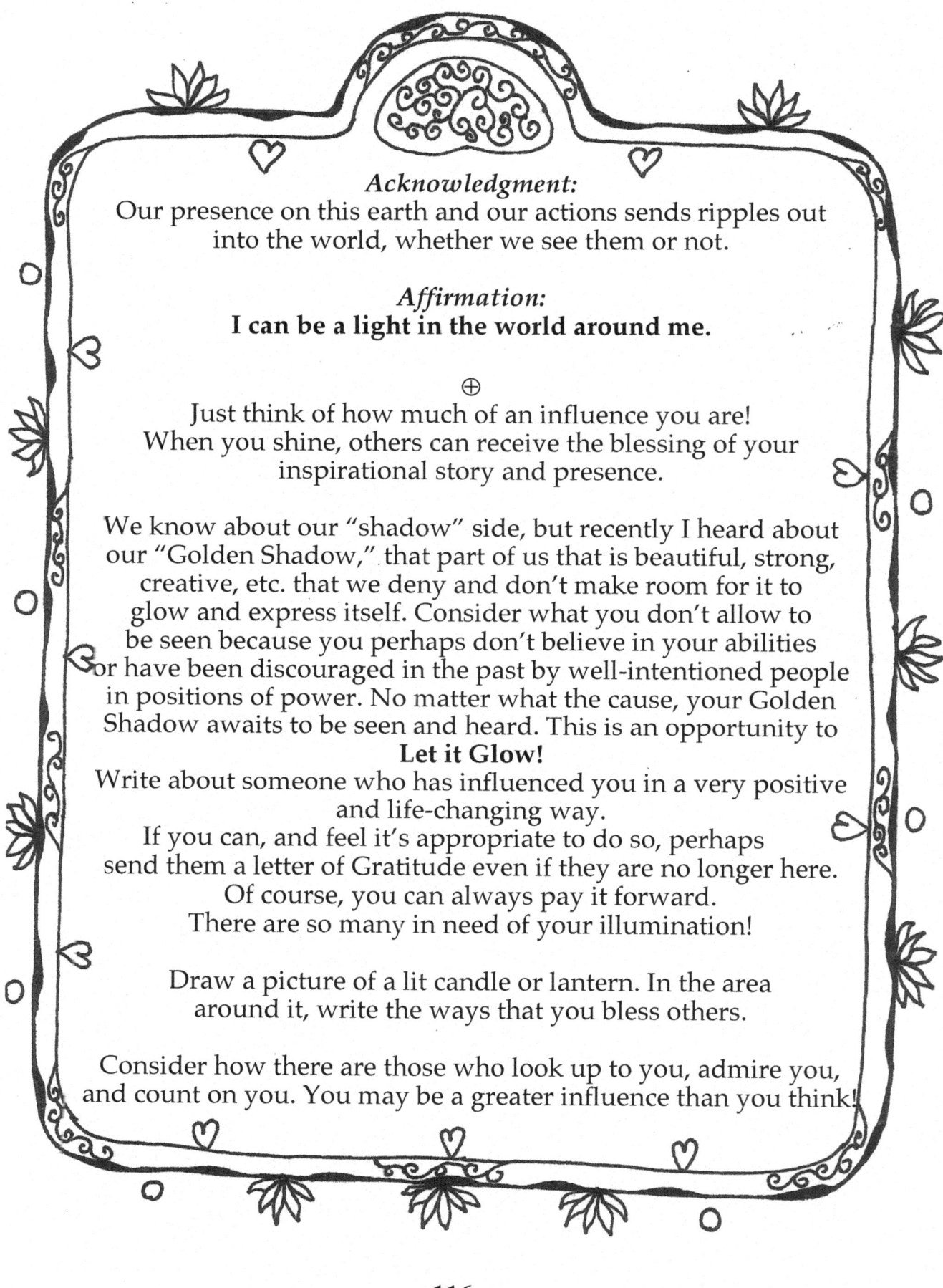

Acknowledgment:
Our presence on this earth and our actions sends ripples out into the world, whether we see them or not.

Affirmation:
I can be a light in the world around me.

⊕

Just think of how much of an influence you are!
When you shine, others can receive the blessing of your inspirational story and presence.

We know about our "shadow" side, but recently I heard about our "Golden Shadow," that part of us that is beautiful, strong, creative, etc. that we deny and don't make room for it to glow and express itself. Consider what you don't allow to be seen because you perhaps don't believe in your abilities or have been discouraged in the past by well-intentioned people in positions of power. No matter what the cause, your Golden Shadow awaits to be seen and heard. This is an opportunity to
Let it Glow!
Write about someone who has influenced you in a very positive and life-changing way.
If you can, and feel it's appropriate to do so, perhaps send them a letter of Gratitude even if they are no longer here.
Of course, you can always pay it forward.
There are so many in need of your illumination!

Draw a picture of a lit candle or lantern. In the area around it, write the ways that you bless others.

Consider how there are those who look up to you, admire you, and count on you. You may be a greater influence than you think!

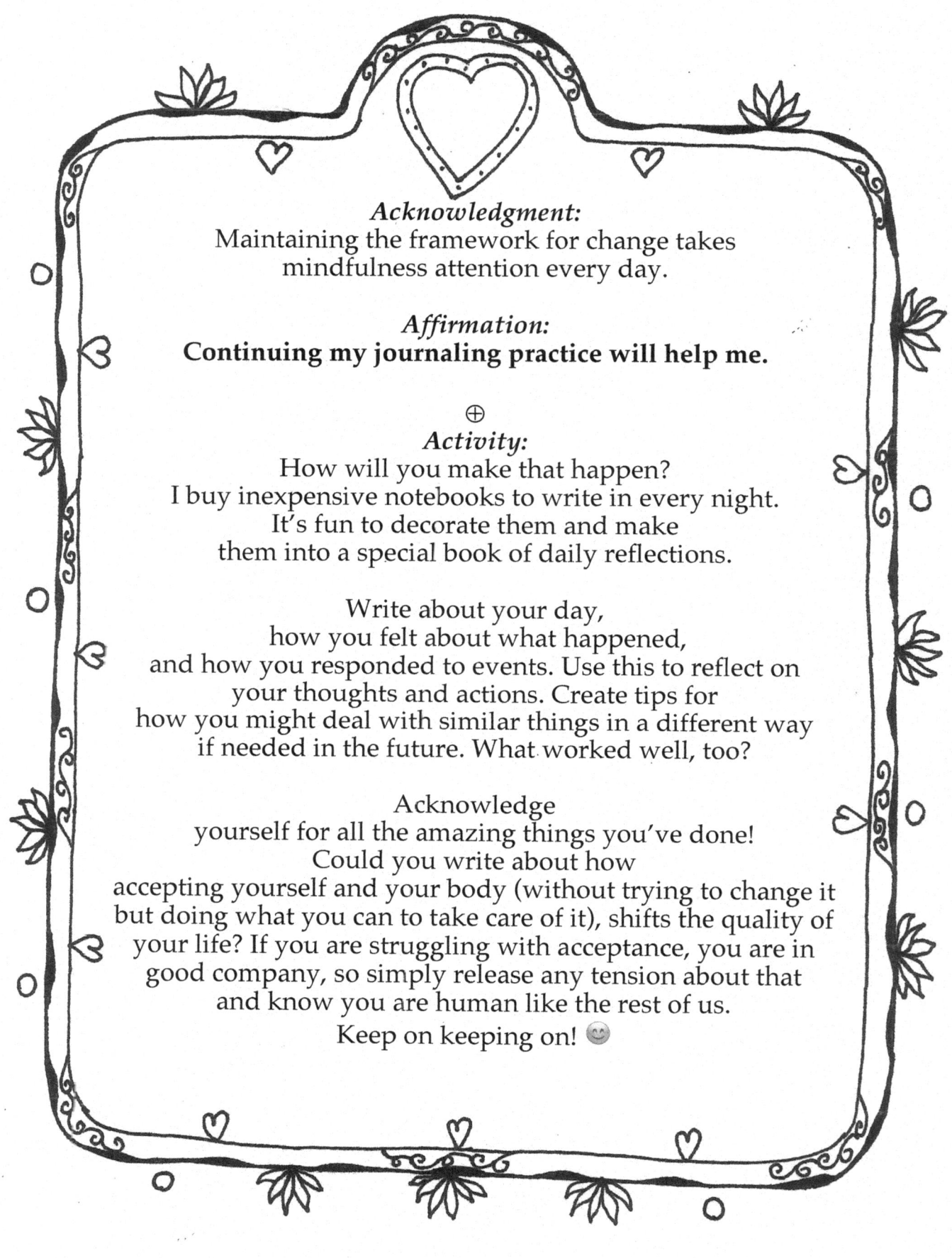

Acknowledgment:
Maintaining the framework for change takes
mindfulness attention every day.

Affirmation:
Continuing my journaling practice will help me.

⊕
Activity:
How will you make that happen?
I buy inexpensive notebooks to write in every night.
It's fun to decorate them and make
them into a special book of daily reflections.

Write about your day,
how you felt about what happened,
and how you responded to events. Use this to reflect on
your thoughts and actions. Create tips for
how you might deal with similar things in a different way
if needed in the future. What worked well, too?

Acknowledge
yourself for all the amazing things you've done!
Could you write about how
accepting yourself and your body (without trying to change it
but doing what you can to take care of it), shifts the quality of
your life? If you are struggling with acceptance, you are in
good company, so simply release any tension about that
and know you are human like the rest of us.
Keep on keeping on! 😊

Congratulations! You've reached
55 days of mindful journaling!

Affirmations:
Taking brave steps towards good health is the start of
a whole new way of living in balance and harmony
with my body, my life, and with the world.
When I feel strong, rested, and well, I am better able to
make a difference in the world.
I can do things I never thought possible, have the stamina
I never thought I had, and fulfill the dreams I thought were
beyond my reach.
All because I took the time to look, listen, accept with love, and
make new choices.

Well Done!!
May you be renewed!

Thank you for taking the time to
join me on this journaling journey.
⊕
What were the most helpful and useful aspects of
using this journal? Use the blank pages at the end of this book to
to continue journaling. ☺
Begin Again.

Acknowledgments

First and always, my heartfelt Gratitude to my beloved husband, Brian Belét for your patient support in all my projects. Thank you for editing and providing feedback in the creation of this journal. beletmusic.com

Thank you to my son, Jacques, for being brave and for your loving support.

Thank you to my beautiful sister Jane Bicquette, for reading through this journal and giving it a "thumbs up".

Much Gratitude to Colleen Campbell for reviewing this journal and for thoughtful feedback.

Thank you to Drs. Krishna Chai (Santa Clara, CA) gastroenterologist of Kaiser Permanente, for your kind help and guidance in managing my sensitive gut, and for your positive thoughts regarding this journal.

Great Thanks to Dr. Gibran Ramos of Portland, Oregon, for your encouragement along with your review.

Heartfelt Gratitude to Manuel Costa, MFT, for your amazing support, feedback, and insightful review.

Thank you to Daniel Davis, MFT, for your feedback and YouTube videos, and to Coleen Ponti-Sarin for your guidance with Psyche-K exercises. Visit Daniel Davis, MFT, website for links to great EMDR and somatic exercise videos. danieldavislmft.com

Aloha e to Stacey Williams, GI nurse at Kaiser, whose compassionate support through a recent flare has my eternal Gratitude.

A Grateful bow to Victoria Navarro Oana for guiding me through somatic and EMDR work.

Mahalo Nui to my friend, Christopher Losa, for the article (see Resources) about low manganese levels and IBD inflammation. coalesce.work

Gratitude to my friend, Myra Kelly, for alerting me to the article about glyphosates and to my friend, Jan Pitcher, for your insights and sharing of helpful information.

Immense Gratitude to Teresa Woodcock for the beautiful book cover. maryterese.com

Heartfelt Gratitude to my family and friends who walk this journey with me.

Marianne's Meta Prayer for IBS and Digestive Disorders/Diseases

May I be well.
May I be in harmony with the
disharmony of my digestive system.
May I love my body and take good care of it.
May I make the best choices for myself so that
I experience less pain.
May I learn to plan, pace, and prioritize my days, making room
for meal planning and preparation.
May I eat mindfully, enjoying every bite.
May I evolve and continue to learn and grow wiser.
May I be grateful to and for my stomach, bowels, and
supportive organs that make it possible for me to live this
Amazing life.

Now, if you are so moved, please extend these wishes to those
you know, strangers, and to all beings. Thank you!

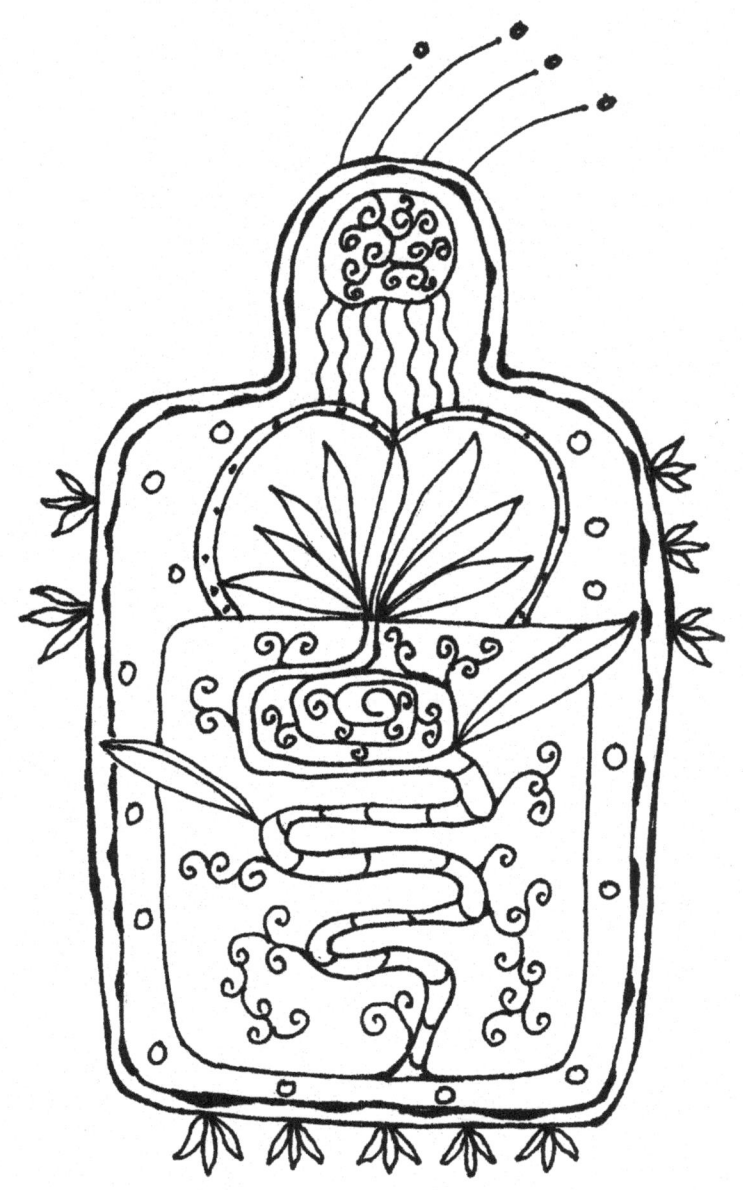

Resources

Check out the Rome Foundation for criteria for IBS.
The Mayo Clinic and Cleveland Clinic both have excellent information on digestive disorders. Also check out IBS Clinics of England.

For Somatic (mind-body) disorders, a helpful source:
The Divided Mind, The Epidemic of Mindbody Disorders by John E Sarno, MD
For understand how trauma is held in the body and how to heal:
The Body Keeps the Score by Bessel Van Der Kolk, MD
And *What It Takes to Heal* by Prentis Hemphill

A technical resource regarding the mind of the gut:
The Second Brain, Your Gut has a Mind of its own by Michael Gershon, MD

Jack Kornfield's Book, *A Path with Heart*, is a great start for anyone interested in learning more about mindfulness and meditation, and Jon Kabat-Zinn's book, *Full Catastrophe Living* is a must read. Also, Pema Chodren's *How to Meditate*, Thich Nhat Hahn's *Moments of Mindfulness,* and Ram Dass's *Journey and Be Here Now* are three great books for beginners.

Dr. Rick Hanson's book, *Neuro Dharma*, is a great read about understanding how the brain works and how to make lasting changes for better health.
www.rickhanson.com
Learn about Polyvagal theory by Dr. Stephen Porges (vagus nerve research and therapy) by visiting: www.stephenporges.com

Belleruth Naparstek is a well-known psychotherapist with numerous *Guided Imagery* programs, physician endorsed, on mind-body connections and managing pain.

The Seeker and the Teacher of Light by Jerry Gin is about my beloved friend, Joachim Wippich. This book is a superb source of healing affirmations.

The Illuminated Rumi Translated by Coleman Barks and Illustrated by Michael Green has *The Guest House* by Rumi with images.

Feeding Your Demons is an insightful read about working with inner monsters by Tsultrim Allione.

Herbal ABC's by Dr. Sharol Marie Tilgner is a superb *Foundation for Herbal Medicine.*
Articles:
Science News Magazine, May 2024 *From the Heart* article by Laura Sanders.
AARP May 2024 Bulletin *The Good Stuff Living Inside You* by Stephen Perrine.
Time Health Winter 2024 *IBD, Six Myths Debunked* by Lindsay Lyon.
Organic Consumers Association. August 2024, *Glyphosate-Based Herbicides Cause Intestinal Damage and Serious Diseases* by Jimese Orange.
Visit *www.futurity.org/maganese-inflammatory* bowel disease by Kim Swine, U- Michigan.

Recommended Cookbooks

The Blue Zone Kitchen by Dan Buettner is a great collection of recipes that were researched and presented in his Netflix series: *The Blue Zone, Live to 100.*

The Acid Watcher Diet by Dr. Jonathan Aviv for reflux flares.

Stress Resilience by Samantha Deere is a little gem of wisdom for living and wonderful recipes.

Becoming Vegan, The Everyday Guide to Plant-Based Nutrition by Brenda Davis, RD, and Vesanto Melina, MS, RD. Not just for vegans! I highly recommend this book for its useful information and charts.

The 30 – Minute Mediterranean Diet by Serena Ball, MS, RDN and Deanna Segrave-Daly, RDN

Easy Ayurveda Cookbook by Rockridge Press.

Vegan World Fusion Cuisine by Mark Reinfeld, Bo Rinaldi, et. al. Infusing the spiritual and art aspects of food making and consuming.

Vegan by Gena Hamshaw. For any kitchen, great plant-based recipes.

Visit *Heather's Tummy Care* for a great cookbook, fiber supplements, teas, and more: www.heatherstummycare.com

Visit www.mountainroseherbs.com for great books like *Alchemy of Herbs* (includes great recipes) by Rosalee De La Forêt, herbs, and more.

For a comprehensive presentation about digestive and overall health: *Digestive Wellness* by Elizabeth Lipski, Ph.D., CCN, CHN

Recommended Netflix Movie:
Hack Your Health: The Secrets of Your Gut (Spring 2024) by Dr. Giulia Enders, who also wrote a book entitled: *Gut, The Inside Story of Our Body's Most Underrated Organ.* This one hour and nineteen-minute movie is informative and fun to watch. Thanks to my sister Jane for the recommendation!

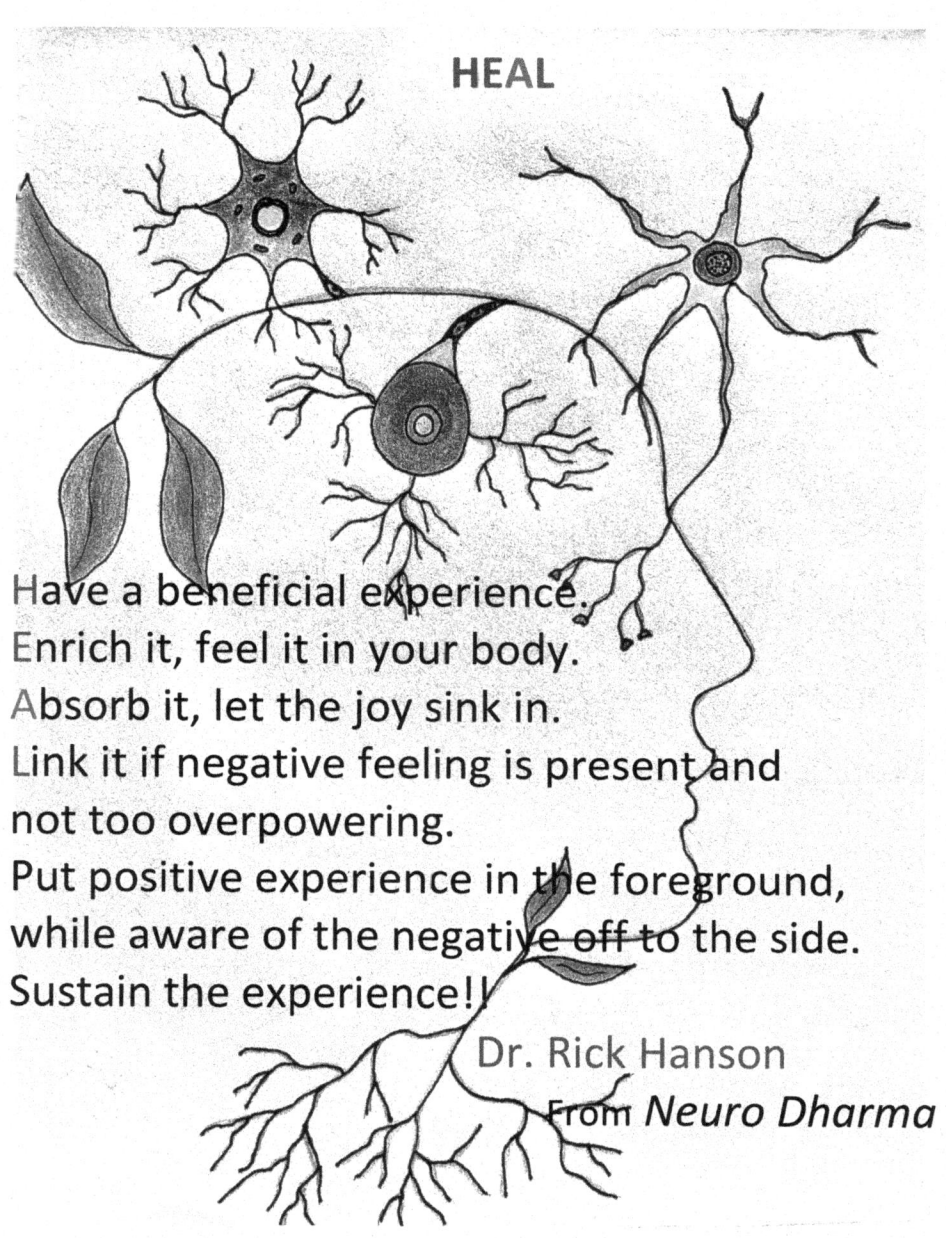

HEAL

Have a beneficial experience.
Enrich it, feel it in your body.
Absorb it, let the joy sink in.
Link it if negative feeling is present and
not too overpowering.
Put positive experience in the foreground,
while aware of the negative off to the side.
Sustain the experience!!

Dr. Rick Hanson
From *Neuro Dharma*

Drawing by Marianne Bickett is featured on Dr. Hanson's website.

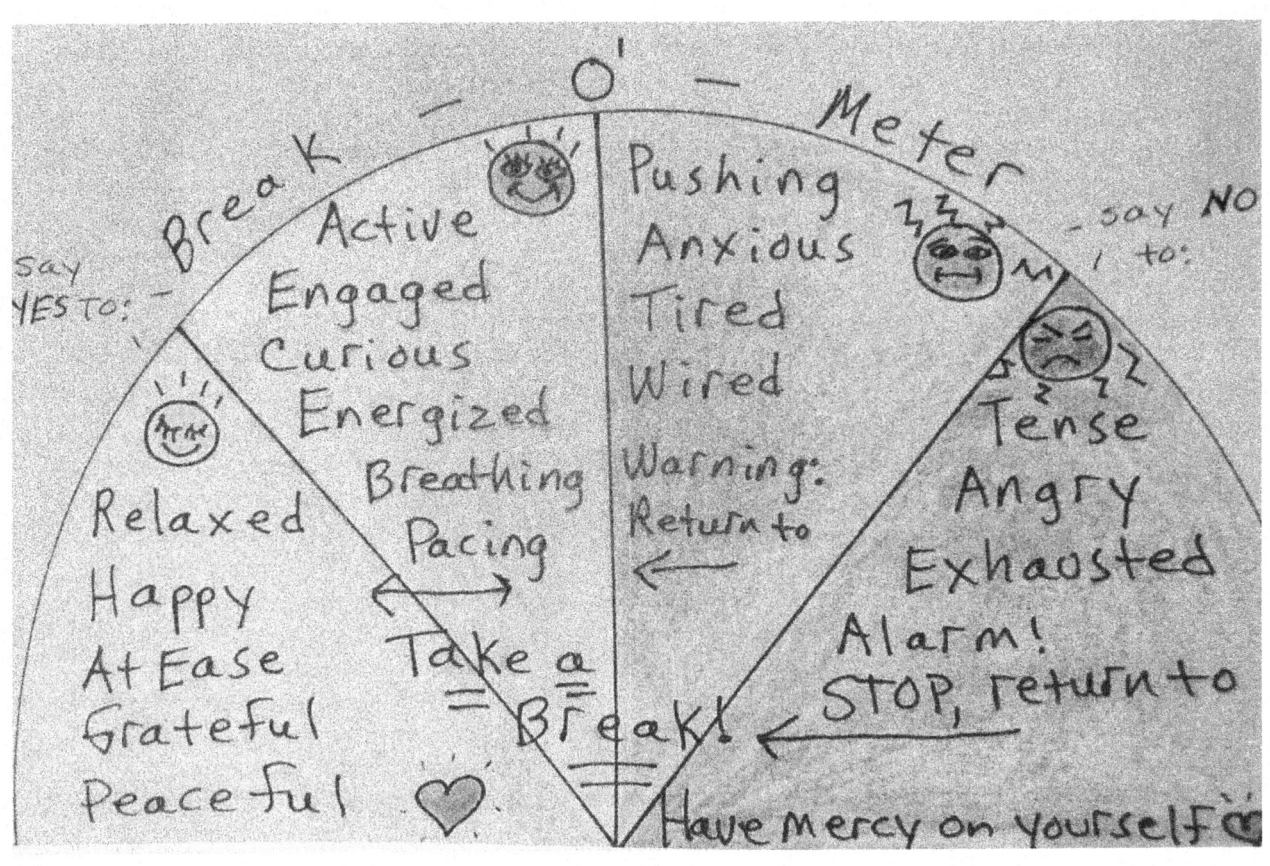

I created this "Break-O-Meter" from Dr. Hanson's *Just One Thing* book in 2018. Since then, I've kept it where I can see it so I can pause and become aware of my energy and state. This has been very helpful in catching myself when I get too close to the red zone!!

Some Things That Have Worked for Me:

I feel I would be remiss in not mentioning some very important practices that have made a huge difference in my lifelong experiences with digestive problems. In addition to mindful eating practices: **First of all, as I've said repeatedly, always consult with your health care practitioner. Secondly, there are herbs and homeopathic remedies that I have used with great success, but always after consultations.** Many of the following are becoming mainstream, however, your doctor may not have the background to endorse their use. Please be sure you are consulting with someone who is knowledgeable about alternative medicine.

As far as **fiber supplements** go, *please consult with your health care provider.* Sometimes it takes a while to find what's best for you. Always introduce any new fiber supplement slowly. I started out with psyllium but found acacia fiber more gentle and helpful. See *Heather's Tummy Care* under Recommended Cookbooks (previous page). Guar gum works for some folks, too. **The best thing is to eat a variety of foods and include lots of veggies!** 😊 *I am purposely not mentioning PPIs nor H2 acid reducers, that is for you and your doctor to address.* Also, there is a specialized diet for SIBO/IMO not listed here. Consider asking your doctor to check your electrolyte/mineral numbers.

For slow motility, space meals/snacks 3 hours apart to allow the stomach to empty. Taking a walk when possible after meals has helped with digestion and it's pleasant!

For stomach acid/reflux problems, I have used these and found them very helpful:
DGL chewable tablets (deglycyrrhizinated licorice extract) I've used for years for flares.
Acidil tablets for relieving heartburn*, and Zinc Carnosine capsules to heal stomach.
Reflux Gourmet, and *Khelp* capsules with alginate can reduce reflux symptoms.
Ginger in cooked food, in tea (fresh or dried) and as gum (for nausea, stomach upset).
Raising the head of the bed six to eight inches to address throat burn* prevention.
*Heartburn and Throat burn are the same thing: when esophagus becomes inflamed.

Teas: *Please consult with a qualified herbalist before using and be aware of any potential allergic reactions as well as contraindications that might interfere with medications you are taking.*
I use only for short periods of time for GERD and IBS symptoms::

Slippery Elm   Marshmallow Root   Plantain   Agrimony

I use the following teas often, either alone or in various combinations, for calming nervous and digestive systems:

Chamomile   Lemon Balm   Oat Tops   Lavender   Holy Basil
          Rose Petals   Fennel seeds   Ginger

Food as Medicine: Again, do not eat anything that may cause a reaction. There are a few recipes on my website. Also, use probiotics upon the advice of your doctor.
Carrot/squash/sweet potato soups with ginger. Broccoli avocado soup (Dr. Aviv).
Okinawa purple sweet potatoes and other sweet potatoes.
Sour Kraut (plain, no garlic, etc) and cabbage juice. Any fermented food like tempeh.
Fennel (bulb) added to dishes, broccoli, zucchini. Artichokes and artichoke soup.
Oatmeal and sourdough bread. Many sourdough white breads have low gluten.
Olive (low heat) and canola oils sparingly. Consult your doctor/dietitian about fats.
Cucumbers (love them sliced, peeled, and in water), Watermelon/melons for heartburn.
Bananas and Papayas, Bosc Pears and Mangoes (non-acidic).
😊

About the Author:

Marianne is a grandmother, retired teacher, author, poet, artist, and lover of life. She enjoys gardening with her grandsons and learning about herbs as well many other interests. Marianne holds a master's degree in art education from the University of Illinois in addition to her bachelor's degree in elementary and special education. She taught for over forty years. Since early childhood, she has dealt with reflux and IBS. Marianne has worked with somatic and Jungian therapists, many specialists, and natural healers, as well as spiritual guides.

For Marianne, the bottom line is:
Regardless of the disease, condition, or illness, our thoughts about our challenges shift everything. We may not be able to change what life has given to us, but we can face it with courage, acceptance, love, creativity, and offer others support. No one needs to experience the pain of IBS or other digestive disorders alone. And it is very possible to alter how you feel by diet and lifestyle changes!

Visit MarianneBickett.com to learn more about her other books and for examples regarding this journal.

The Starfish Story

This beautiful story may be well-known these days, but it bears repeating.

Once there was a man walking along the beach. The shore was covered with starfish that were deposited on the beach after a storm. The starfish were dying for lack of water.

The man looked at all the starfish and began to toss one starfish at a time back into the sea.

Another person approached him and said, "What are you doing? You are wasting your time. There are too many starfish. What you are doing won't matter."

The man picked up another starfish and tossed it into the water. He looked at the stranger, saying, "It mattered to that one."

You matter. Your choices matter.

Author's End Note

The Hawaiian word for gut is **na'au*** and it encompasses not only the gut but also the heart and mind in the realm of emotions. It's about relationships and connections between emotions and these vital organs.

To be clear, I still have GERD and IBS. Despite my awareness and experiences along with wonderful support, things happen. Sometimes I can easily pinpoint the trigger and other times I'm left puzzled. A recent electrolyte imbalance, for example, was causing nausea until I connected the dots. Also, reducing oils, especially at night, has really helped my GERD. Once the physical reason for the problem is resolved, cultivating a healthy relationship with our bodies, especially our gut, builds a resiliency for those times when reoccurrences happen.

Hypersensitivity can lead to pain and discomfort even after the cause has been healed. Sometimes the "loop" between the brain and gut keeps firing despite the reason no longer existing. That's where interoception and mindfulness can really help. We can settle the reactivity as we become aware of what's going on. Working with the mind, spirit, emotions, and physical natures makes sense; as I mentioned at the beginning of this book, everything is related. To address only one aspect of an illness makes little sense. Our bodies never lie, as my wise sister Pat used to say.

There is mounting evidence that the pesticides we use on our food are making us sick. Even washing fruit and vegetables hasn't proven to keep the residue of glyphosates out of our bodies. Glyphosates have been strongly indicated as a cause of a huge increase in digestive diseases and disorders. Check out a recent article by the **Organic Consumers Association**. Write to your legislators and urge them to ban the use of pesticides, particularly those with glyphosates. We shouldn't be using pesticides at all. Period. Also, the science is clear about the plastic in our blood and in our organs. We need to drastically reduce the amount of plastic we use that ends up in our food and in our water. (see my website under the *Plastic Pollution* tab). Currently, scientists are attempting to understand the threat to our health from the plastic in our bodies. Refuse, Reduce, Repurpose, Recycle!

I am deeply Grateful to live in harmony with this beloved body where I dwell and call my home. May you, too, feel at home in your body and at peace.

*www.hawaii.edu/news/2022/11/29/hawaiian-word-of-the-week-naau/

This chart is based on Dr. Aviv's *Acid Watcher Diet* book (see **Resources**) that recommends five mini meals a day, but for slow motility like I have, you may need to space 3 hours between meals/snacks. Of course, use this with guidance. Feel free to alter this chart in any way that serves you.

Menu for the Week

Mon.	Tues.	Wed.	Thur.	Fri.

NOTES:

Embodiment

I sing from the hollows of my being,
through the windswept chambers of my heart,
through the canyons of my bowels,
through the trees of my veins and arteries.
I listen from the rivers of my blood,
into the folds of my brain,
into the vision of my sight.
I birth and die the cells of my house that
return return to the mossy dirt, and
fall again again from the cloud of me.
I dance among the fields of my skin,
among the singing, among the wailing and the laughing
of this universe. I am
lightyears and moments melded
into the vast undiscovered spaces
of my body beautiful, breathing,
wonderfully ephemeral, lovingly tended,
and wildly unknown.

©2024 Marianne Bickett

Live Well.

A Parting Gift

I have a jar on my desk where I began to place special,
little items that I found that were beautiful or meaningful.
Things like a small blue stone, a wooden bead, and even
a dime I found on a walk. After a time, I realized I was creating
a sort of "treasure box" like the ones my grandsons have.
When I see my little treasure
jar and the colorful items inside, I feel content and grateful.
This small thing has become a kind of support for
my well-being and reminds me what a treasure life is.
What would you put in a treasure jar or box? Could you create one?

Thank you!
MarianneBickett.com